LITERARY LANDSCAPES

LITERARY LANDSCAPES

Walking Tours in
Great Britain and Ireland

L. N. Franco

GEORGE BRAZILLER PUBLISHER   NEW YORK

First published by George Braziller, Inc. in 1998

Library of Congress Cataloging-in-Publication Data:

Franco, L. N.
    Literary landscapes : walking tours in Great Britain and Ireland /
L. N. Franco.—1st ed.
        p.   cm.
    Includes bibliographical references.
    ISBN 0-8076-1438-6 (pbk.)
    1. Literary landmarks—Great Britain—Guidebooks. 2. Authors,
English—Homes and haunts—England—Guidebooks. 3. Authors, Irish
—Homes and haunts—Ireland—Guidebooks. 4. Literary landmarks
—Ireland—Guidebooks. 5. Landscape—Great Britain—Guidebooks.
6. Walking—Great Britain—Guidebooks. 7. Landscape—Ireland
—Guidebooks. 8. Walking—Ireland—Guidebooks.   I. Title.
PR109.F67   1998
820.9—dc21
                                                           98–39502
                                                           CIP

For information, please address the publisher:
George Braziller, Inc.
171 Madison Avenue
New York, NY 10016

Photographs by L. N. Franco
Maps by Rita Lascaro
Designed by Philip Grushkin
Printed and bound in the United States

First edition

To Marie,
my faithful navigator and dedicated walker

My thanks to Valerie Walker and Mary Taveras for a beyond-the-pale editing job and to George Braziller for his vision. I am grateful to Rita Lascaro, who drew the maps, for her sharp eye for detail and accuracy. I would also like to thank my Pasadena City College semester-abroad students for their sympathetic imaginations.

CONTENTS

Introduction 13

1. THE WORDSWORTHS' LAKE DISTRICT 19

2. THE BRONTËS' MOORS 33

3. D. H. LAWRENCE'S MIDLANDS 47

4. LEWIS CARROLL'S OXFORD 59

5. THOMAS HARDY'S DORSET 71

6. JANE AUSTEN'S BATH 84

7. DYLAN THOMAS'S WALES 93

8. JAMES JOYCE'S DUBLIN 106

9. YEATS'S WESTERN IRELAND 124

Additional Travel Information 141

Glossary 145

Selected Bibliography 147

Acknowledgments 151

INTRODUCTION

On my latest trip to Dublin, I did what I usually do on the night I arrive in town: I dropped in for a pint at Davy Byrnes's "moral pub," as it's called in James Joyce's *Ulysses*. I took a stool at the bar, ordered my pint, and settled in to soak up the ambience. It soon became obvious, though, that I was the one being carefully sized up. After a few moments an old, gnarled, gap-toothed fellow a few stools away said, "Now let me guess. American, schoolteacher, here to do the Joyce thing." (He pronounced "thing" more like "ting.")

I smiled. "Well, yes, sort of. I come here fairly often." I was already on the defensive—not a good position to be in, in an Irish pub.

"Bloom, Leo Bloom, came here."

"Yes, I know." I tried to cut him short.

"You got it all wrong, you know."

"What?" I asked, and immediately I realized I had fallen into his trap.

"For a pint now I'll tell you the real story and where he sat."

"I'll buy you the pint," I replied, "but I know that Bloom was just a fictional character." I hoped that would hold him. I noticed the bartender had already begun drawing a pint of Guinness for the old codger—I had been set up. The Irish are great storytellers; all they need is an audience, and I had unwittingly become an audience of one for what was clearly an ongoing drama at this pub.

"Fictional-smictional, he came in here all right," the old man said as he waited for his Guinness. "Sat over there at the small table near the door. He wasn't Irish, you know."

"How do you know? Did you read the book?"

"That booook! That dirty booook! Never! I just know. He was not a Dublin man. You'd know that if you knew what he ate and drank."

"I do know—Gorgonzola cheese sandwich and red wine." He had me now.

"See, what'd I tell ya, a Dublin man would never order an Eye-talian cheese, or is it Spanish? He'd order a good Irish cheddar if it comes to that. And wine? Ha! With this here made right here in Dublin." He took a long draft of his Guinness. "Now that's a drink for you, American."

"But he was a Dublin man," I protested. "The book . . ."

"Pshaaaw! The booook! That's all you Americans talk about."

I was relieved to see three young Americans come in and stand between me and my tormentor. The old codger gave me a sly wink and turned to address them.

"I'll bet you're Americans, here for that Joyce booook," he started.

They laughed and fell into his trap just as easily as I had. "Why, yes, we are," said one of the Americans.

I couldn't bear to go through it all over again so I gave him a nod and headed for the door. As I left, I looked back. The bartender was drawing him another pint of Guinness.

While my exchange with the old codger hardly qualifies as a serious discussion of Joyce's *Ulysses,* I've probably talked about as much literature in Irish, English, Welsh, and Scottish pubs as I have in my college classes. The Irish may refer to Joyce's *Ulysses* as "that dirty book," but they are convinced that "Joyce was better than Shakespeare and the English know it," as one pub regular put it. In Laugharne, Wales, Dylan Thomas's hometown, a fisherman once lectured me for three hours on how Thomas's play *Under Milk Wood* shows that Thomas really wanted to be a sea captain-poet. And in Haworth someone I met in the Black Bull—the pub frequented by Branwell, the brother of the Brontë sisters—invited me to walk the moors after midnight, when the ghosts of Cathy and Heathcliff might be spotted roaming the hills behind Top Withens, the supposed site of Wuthering Heights. "Fictional-smictional," as the Irish codger remarked. Through the prism of literature, as Joyce called it, fact and fiction become inextricably intertwined.

Literary Landscapes is about reading and walking. While the works I've featured here are products of the authors' imaginations, they are also deeply grounded in the reality of a specific place. *Literary Landscapes* highlights the connections among actual settings, the imagination of the writers, and the settings' ultimate depiction in their writing. Not all literature, of course, is enhanced by firsthand knowledge of its setting. Experiencing a setting is only one aspect of a deeper appreciation of the writing. Yet the settings of some works seem to invite a visit more than others. It is this thought that guided me in making the selections for this book. The idea is to read, walk, and muse over what you have read. I have found this to be the best way to form lasting images of the places I've been and the books I've read.

Since there are so many great English and Irish writers from which to choose, how did I select the writers in this collection? First, I focused on those who chose actual and identifiable settings for their works. I then narrowed the selection to those settings that are accessible to visitors today. I also sought out a combination of writers whose settings provide the greatest scenic variety. The contrast, for example, between walking in the lush, green countryside of the Lake District reading about dancing daffodils one day and hiking in the stark, foreboding moors of the Brontë sisters reading about death and decay the next is both striking and delightful. I avoided writers who set their works in London and spent most of their time there, as a number of literary tours of that city are already available. Shakespeare requires volumes of his own, so he, too, has been excluded. Other writers are not included because their fictional settings are no longer accessible.

Each chapter opens with a brief biographical sketch of the writer and his or her connection to a particular place. Some of the more controversial events in their lives are recounted as well as still debated issues about them. Next, the actual walks in and around the literary sites are described and illustrated with maps (maps of walks in the cities of Eastwood, Oxford, and Dublin are not provided as many excellent maps of these areas are already available). Several of the walks involve some driving to and from sites, and one of them can also be taken by boat instead of by foot.

The maps provided here are intended as general guides only. For more detailed maps, I recommend the British Ordnance Survey Landranger Series— all-purpose maps that show public rights-of-way. For a listing of the maps in the series that apply to the areas described here, see the selected bibliography. Also in the back is a glossary of terms for numerous British-English words used throughout the book as well as additional travel information that provides further details about the sites visited in the walks.

A good number of the settings described here were written about by writers who no longer lived in the very places they evoke with such accuracy and sensitivity. Joyce wrote *Ulysses* while living in Paris. William Butler Yeats was inspired to write "The Lake Isle of Innisfree" while in London. D. H. Lawrence wrote three novels about Eastland while living in London and Cornwall. A literary landscape, then, tells us much about a writer's memory of place and shows how memory both distorts and recalls through the haze of nostalgia and distance.

The reader who travels to the sites once frequented by the author not only learns more about the author, but also about the characters and stories invented by the author. I once led a group of American college students on a study-abroad program in Oxford, England. We were reading Emily Brontë's *Wuthering Heights* and chartered a bus to take us to West Yorkshire to visit Keighley (pronounced *keethly*) Moor, the supposed setting of the novel. Most of the students had never seen moorlands. As we neared Yorkshire, the noise on the bus reached peak levels with loud chattering and blaring rock music. We crested a hill and suddenly found ourselves surrounded by moorland—stark, treeless, barren, and foreboding. The landscape was one from a Brontë novel: windy, threatening skies with heavy, ominous-looking clouds scudding across them, an occasional clap of thunder, and though only two in the afternoon, it was as dark as it was dreary. The chattering stopped, the music was turned off, and the mood on the bus transformed as the students sat staring off into that strange and, to them, desolate landscape. They were mesmerized by it.

Later, in a steady, cold rain, as we walked the moors to Top Withens, two dark and huddled figures came over the rise ahead of us. We held our breath.

Brontë's work had so taken hold of our imaginations that we half expected to meet the ghosts of Cathy and Heathcliff on the moors.

For the sheer pleasure of walks in the countryside, it is difficult to do better than Dorset through the eyes of Thomas Hardy. You can find the lanes traveled by Bathsheba Everdene of *Far from the Madding Crowd,* walk on the Egdon Heath of *The Return of the Native,* and hear the hymns in village churches that were sung some hundred years ago. Hardy is a genius at re-creating place. But then so is Lawrence. He is to the Midlands of England what Hardy is to Dorset. Lawrence's Midlands, however, are industrial, dotted with the ruins of coal mines as reminders of the devastating rape of the landscape. Lawrence's country is the most unpredictable in England. A country walk can lead right to a power plant or the ruins of a school or mill. This is the landscape Lawrence wrote about with deep passion, the world he both loved and hated.

It is less than 100 miles as the crow flies from *Wuthering Heights's* Keighley Moor to Windermere, the heart of the Lake District. Yet it is light years away in terms of landscape, and we see that difference in the writings of Dorothy and William Wordsworth. While suffering and poverty are described in some of William's poems and in Dorothy's journals, hope and an emphasis on renewal are the dominant themes—concepts difficult to find in the more tragic vision of the Brontës.

Jane Austen's Bath and Charles Lutwidge Dodgson's (a.k.a. Lewis Carroll) Oxford are both delightful to experience on foot. Bath is a small, magnificent city that preserves many of the popular social spots of Austen's time. Oxford, though somewhat frenetic, can be experienced much in the same manner that Dodgson did. This is the city where he met Alice Liddell, and where as a don (or lecturer) in mathematics at Christ Church he wrote the splendidly fanciful *Alice's Adventures in Wonderland.* As an observant trip up the Thames and around Oxford will show you, his fantasies were steeped in the life of nineteenth-century Oxford.

There is perhaps no better means of attaining insight into Yeats's mysticism (short of reading him, of course) than to walk in a driving rain in western Ireland, climb the flat-topped mountain Knocknarea, and arrive, drenched, at the so-called tomb of Queen Maeve. Contrast this experience with that of Joyce's Leopold Bloom in *Ulysses,* who wanders about a sharply realistic Dublin knowing his wife is in bed with another man.

To walk the estuary path in Laugharne, Wales, while reading Dylan Thomas's poems aloud is perhaps the most fulfilling walking experience of all. I once did this and heard my words echo behind me. I turned to see a young woman reciting the same poem, but from memory, and walking with a surer-footed knowledge of the path as well.

The English poet John Keats described a romantic as someone with a sympathetic imagination. If we add to that the desire to journey, to experience firsthand what these writers and poets felt, saw, and thought, we are transformed into the adventurer of Alfred, Lord Tennyson's poem "Ulysses":

> . . . Come, my friends,
> 'Tis not too late to seek a newer world.
> Push off, and sitting well in order smite
> The sounding furrows; for my purpose holds
> To sail beyond the sunset, and the baths
> Of all the western stars, until I die.
> . . .
> To strive, to seek, to find, and not to yield.

Profound changes are taking place in the landscape of the British Isles. The British and the Irish are trying to preserve the sites I've written about here, but when one sees wind turbines on the moors and new housing tracts springing up around Dorchester, a sense of urgency prevails. Travelers must pack their books and their bags and set sail. For as any good reader knows, reading is not a passive process, but rather an active one requiring an alert and open mind willing to discourse with the author. Walking enhances this process and adds new dimensions to what we have read.

1

The Wordsworths' Lake District

*In preparing this Manual, it was the Author's principal
wish to furnish a Guide or Companion for the Minds of
Persons of taste, and feeling for Landscape, who might be
inclined to explore the District of the Lakes with that
degree of attention to which its beauty may fairly lay claim.*

—WILLIAM WORDSWORTH, *Guide to the Lakes*

The Lake District in northwest England has been called the most beautiful corner of England. Located in present-day Cumbria County, some 250 miles north of London, virtually the entire area (about 35 square miles) has been designated a national park. It is a walker's paradise and is known for England's nineteenth-century Lake Poets, primarily William Wordsworth, Samuel Taylor Coleridge, and Robert Southey. William (1770–1850) is the most famous of the poets. He and his sister Dorothy Wordsworth (1771–1855), were born in the District, where their father was a business agent for an earl of Lonsdale, and lived there all their lives.

The Lake District trails are best walked with a volume of William's works, his *Selected Poems and Prefaces*, for example, and his *Description of the Scenery of the Lakes in the North of England,* a sort of tourist guidebook of its day (first published in 1822) now available as *Guide to the Lakes.* Dorothy's *Grasmere Journals* also makes excellent accompaniment. The combination of her straightforward descriptions and William's fanciful images transform these walks into journeys both meditative and instructive.

Dorothy's journals are wonderful. She is not afraid to express her passionate love for the fells, becks, crags, tarns, meres, flowers, woods, and the countless other natural features of the pastoral landscape. Grasmere, for which her journal is named, is the tiny village by the lake where she and her brother lived from 1799 to 1808 in a small, simple country house known as Dove Cottage. This is where William composed much of his best-known nature poetry. He and Dorothy lived alone in the cottage until William married in 1802.

Dorothy transcribed poetry for her brother and spent many hours reading with him. She herself possessed great talent, but as her journals reveal, she devoted her life to her brother's writing. Her dedication to his genius is clearly documented in her own words: she explains that she kept a journal "because [she] shall give William pleasure by it." Dorothy never married and remained with her brother until his death. William recognized her dedication and valued it immensely. As he wrote in a letter to a friend, "She gave me eyes, she gave me ears."

Dorothy and William clearly loved each other deeply. Whether they shared an incestuous relationship, as town gossip would have it, however, is another question. William and Dorothy were known to take long walks together in the mountains and, upon parting, were seen to kiss each other ardently. Thomas De Quincey, the writer and a dear friend of the Wordsworths, defended them in a letter to one of the townspeople saying that this was normal for William, who kissed all women, be they relatives or not, upon parting.

Their relationship is perhaps best understood through their own words. William describes it in his poem "Lines Composed a Few Miles Above Tintern Abbey," published in 1798:

Figure 1. Dove Cottage. Town End, Grasmere Village, Cumbria.

> For thou art with me here upon the banks
> Of this fair river; thou my dearest Friend,
> My dear, dear Friend, and in thy voice I catch
> The language of my former heart, and read
> My former pleasures in the shooting lights
> Of thy wild eyes. Oh! yet a little while
> May I behold in thee what I was once,
> My dear, dear Sister!

William's marriage to Mary Hutchinson in 1802 profoundly affected Dorothy. Although she went to Yorkshire for the wedding, she did not attend the ceremony. Her riot of emotions over her brother's marriage is described in her journal: "I gave him the wedding ring—with how deep a blessing! I took it from my forefinger where I had worn it the whole of the night before—he slipped it again onto my finger and blessed me fervently." When William arrived home from his wedding, not with Mary but with one of his brothers, Dorothy wrote:

> I kept myself as quiet as I could, but when I saw the two men
> running up the walk, coming to tell us it [the wedding] was
> over, I could stand it no longer and threw myself on the bed,
> where I lay in stillness, neither hearing nor seeing anything till
> Sara came upstairs to me and said "They are coming." This
> forced me from the bed where I lay and I moved I know not
> how straight forward, faster than my strength could carry me
> till I met my beloved William and fell upon his bosom.

William now had two women devoted to him and the fostering of his talent. The women did their best to keep him from being disturbed by the strenuous, time-consuming duties of running a household in rather primitive circumstances. On sunny days William sat in the garden writing, while the women did the washing and ironing, tended the fire, and did the baking and cooking. Amid all these responsibilities, Dorothy still found time to keep her journal, converse with William and Coleridge, and go on long evening walks.

The Wordsworths—who now included three children William and Mary had had—left Dove Cottage in 1808 for Allen Bank, a larger house northwest of Grasmere. This new house was drafty and uncomfortable and the Wordworths were unhappy there; William called it a "temple of Abomination." Their lease expired in 1811 and they happily left Allen Bank for the Rectory in Grasmere. This house, however, also proved unsatisfactory. Then, in 1813, William was offered an annual gift of £100, a large sum at that time, from a patron of his poetry, Lord Lonsdale (he was probably from the same family as the earl for whom William's father had worked). This sum, plus William's appointment as distributor of stamps (a duty charged for validating legal documents) for what was then the County of Westmorland at £400 per year, allowed them to rent a larger home, Rydal Mount, just two miles from Dove Cottage and overlooking the lake called Rydal Water. It is a spacious old farmhouse that was expanded before the Wordsworths moved in. Later, the Wordsworths expanded it even more by adding another story. The house was now large enough to accommodate their growing family and their friends.

With the passing of time, life at Rydal Mount became increasingly difficult for Dorothy. She always had problems with her teeth and suffered from severe headaches, which today would be diagnosed as migraines. To ease her pain, Dorothy was prescribed laudanum, an opium-based drug popular in her day. She suffered a debilitating intestinal illness in 1829 and grew weaker and weaker until she was confined to her bedroom on the second floor of the house, where William and Mary looked after her. She had periods of violent behavior when she shouted obscenities and failed to recognize her beloved brother and sister-in-law. Today her condition would probably be recognized as dementia and perhaps Alzheimer's disease. William himself became ill in the late 1840s and died in 1850. Dorothy had momentary periods of awareness but was slipping steadily toward death, which came in 1855. Mary died at Rydal Mount in 1859.

Whereas William's poetry was published during his lifetime, Dorothy insisted that her journals remain private for her and her brother's use only. *The Grasmere Journals* were first published in 1958 and cover the period from 1800 to 1803. Her journals, which will serve as our primary guide to the Lake District as it was known by the Wordsworths, contain images that William used in some of his poetry. One of his more beloved poems, "I Wandered Lonely as a Cloud," owes much of its descriptive beauty to Dorothy's observations. While on an outing to a nearby lake called Ullswater, Dorothy came upon some daffodils along the lake shore. She wrote in her journal:

> I never saw daffodils so beautiful . . . some rested their heads
> upon these stones as on a pillow for weariness; and the rest
> tossed and reeled and danced and seemed as if they verily
> laughed with the wind that blew upon them over the lake; they
> looked so gay ever glancing ever changing.

Her brother borrows this imagery to open his poem:

> I wandered lonely as a cloud
> That floats on high o'er vales and hills,
> When all at once I saw a crowd,
> A host, of golden daffodils;
> Beside the lake, beneath the trees,
> Fluttering and dancing in the breeze.

William and Dorothy clearly drew on each other for inspiration in their writing.

It is Dorothy's diary, however, that offers fresher, more immediate insights. Her beautiful writing rivals her brother's poetry. She describes, for instance, an autumn morning in 1802:

There was a most lovely combination at the head of the vale of
the yellow autumnal hills wrapped in sunshine and overhung
with partial mists, the green and yellow trees and the snow-
topped mountains. It was a most heavenly morning.

Such writing belies the everyday difficulties of her life. The Wordsworths lived
under conditions that would be hard for most of us to imagine today, and they
witnessed life's tragedies firsthand. The realities of starvation; homelessness; dis-
eases that maimed and killed with little warning; poor communications; long dis-
tances to travel for necessities; and heavy, physical labor just to eat, drink, and
stay warm formed part of their everyday lives. Dorothy wrote of these extreme
difficulties in a direct manner, leaving us with a strong impression of rural England in the early 1800s. In a particularly poignant passage she writes, "The snow
still lies upon the ground. . . . I heard a cart pass the door and at the same time
the dismal sound of a crying infant." In another place she writes:

As we came up the White Moss we met an old man, who I saw
was a beggar by his two bags hanging over his shoulder, but
from a half laziness, half indifference and a wanting to try him
if he would speak I let him pass. He said nothing and my heart
smote me. I turned back and said You are begging? 'Ay', says he.
I gave him a halfpenny.

In addition to her observations of nature and the inhabitants of the Lake District, Dorothy reveals much about the lives of the Lake District poets and De
Quincey, the writer. Coleridge, for instance, visited them often, and her journals provide some amusing details about his visits to Grasmere. One day, he was
attacked by a cow. "Coleridge came in with a sack full of books and a branch of
mountain ash, he had been attacked by a cow—he came over by Grisedale—a
furious wind." Another time he carved his initials on a rock near Helvellyn:

We parted from Coleridge at Sara's Crag after having looked at
the letters Coleridge carved in the morning. I kissed them all.
William deepened the T with Coleridge's penknife. We sate
afterwards on the wall, seeing the sun go down and the reflec-
tions in the still water. Coleridge looked well and parted from
us cheerfully, hopping up upon the Side stones.

Unfortunately, the rock with Coleridge's initials was blasted to widen the
road, but a monument of its fragments remains. It is just across the Ambleside road where the road passes Thirlmere Lake, about three miles north of
Grasmere.

Coleridge and Dorothy walked the paths and lanes together, sometimes with
William and others, but often just the two of them. She was fond of Coleridge,
and there was talk of romance between them. Rydal Water and Grasmere certainly provide an ideal setting for romantic moonlit walks. She looked forward

to his visits and was familiar with his poetry and deep philosophical bent. Whatever romantic feelings she may have had toward him she never wrote about. Later, their relationship took an unfortunate turn when the Wordsworths felt Coleridge was abusing opium. His appearance on a visit to their home in 1806 so shocked Dorothy that she wrote in a letter, "His fatness has quite changed him—it's more like the flesh of a person in dropsy than in health."

Much of the natural splendor described by Dorothy and immortalized by her brother nearly two hundred years ago can be enjoyed by the visitor who takes pleasure in country walks. Views abound of sweeping valleys dotted with sheep, gray-stone cottages, smoke puffing up out of chimneys even in July, lakes, streams, and waterfalls in a valley protected by high rolling hills and craggy mountains. More shades of green exist in the Lake District than anywhere else in the world. To see daffodils such as Dorothy described, one must arrive in early spring; they usually reach full bloom by early April.

There are hundreds of walks, from very easy lakeside strolls to strenuous rock and crag climbing. The British revere their footpaths, and these crisscross the district. A footpath safeguards a walker's right-of-way whether it crosses public or private land.

As you follow Dorothy's footsteps, you might consider what a remarkable feat her walks were: she frequently forded streams, cut across boggy bottomland, and kept her balance on snow- and ice-covered paths. Whatever path your thoughts take as you walk in the Lake District, Dorothy's *Grasmere Journals* will greatly enrich your experience, whether you see "Rydale [Rydal Water] with a sullen face" or "the north sky . . . fading into pale blue & streaked & scattered over with steady islands of purple melting away into shades of pink. . . ."

WORDSWORTH WALK 1, *The Lake District*

Sites Featured: Dove Cottage, John's Grove, Rydal Mount, and the step-ping-stones across the River Rothay. *Distance:* About 5 miles depending on side excursions and choice of return route. *Degree of Difficulty:* Easy. *Time:* About 4 hours. *Starting Point:* Dove Cottage. *See Map.*

Follow the narrow, paved road from Dove Cottage up a slight hill to the old Gras-mere-Rydal Road. You'll come to John's Grove, a thick grove of beech trees. John Wordsworth, one of William and Dorothy's three brothers, stayed with them for nine months in 1800, and the three Wordsworths walked often in this wood, also referred to by the Wordsworths as the firgrove. John, a seaman, was lost at sea soon after this visit, and William renamed the grove after his brother. While still awaiting John's return, William wrote a poem called "The Fir-grove" from which these lines are excerpted:

> At a short distance from my cottage, stands
> A stately Fir-grove, whither I was wont
> To hasten, for I found beneath the roof
> Of that perennial shade, a cloistral place
> Of refuge, with an unencumbered floor.
> . . .
> The fir-grove murmurs with a sea-like sound,
> Alone I tread this path;—for aught I know,
> Timing my steps to thine; and with a store
> Of undistinguishable sympathies,
> Mingling most earnest wishes for the day
> When we, and others whom we love, shall meet
> A second time, in Grasmere's happy Vale.

Walk through John's Grove and follow the upper road to White Moss Tarn. Some speculate that this is where Dorothy and William met a leech gatherer mentioned in her journal: "We met an old man almost double . . . his trade was to gather leeches, but now leeches are scarce and he had not the strength for it. . . ." William depicted him in his poem "Resolution and Independence": "I saw a man before me unawares/The oldest man he seemed that ever wore grey hairs."

Continue along the road until it joins the footpath to Rydal. This area was one of Dorothy's favorite to walk in and you can see why; even though it is under a craggy knoll called Nab Scar, it still has a clear view of both lakes, Grasmere and Rydal Water. To Dorothy this was a magical place. She often came here on moonlit nights alone or with her brother to sit and spend quiet moments on the hillside. An journal entry of 1800 includes this passage:

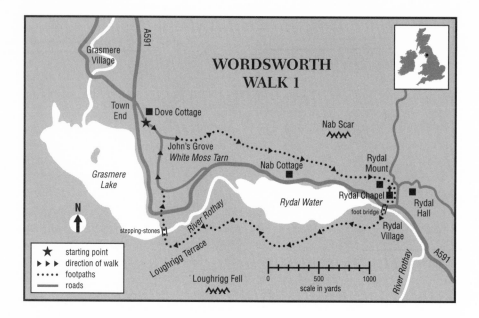

We walked to Rydale [Rydal] to inquire for letters. We walked
over the hill by the firgrove. I sate upon a rock, and observed a
flight of swallows gathering together high over my head. . . .
The lake of Rydale very beautiful, partly still. . . . There was a
curious yellow reflection in the water, as of corn fields. There
was no light in the clouds from which it appeared to come.

Continue along the path with Rydal Water on your right and Nab Scar towering above on your left. This path leads directly to Rydal Mount, a large stately
home surrounded by gardens and a soft green lawn that slopes down toward the
lake. Stroll through the gardens overlooking the water. William saw himself as
something of a landscape gardener, and he designed the terraces and the gardens, including the kitchen garden where they grew cabbages, carrots, and
other vegetables. William, Dorothy, and Mary walked these terraces, and as there
were few trees, they had grand views of the lakes and the mountains across from
them. William also increased the size of a Norse mound (a burial ground) in order
to climb up on it and achieve more sweeping views. The mound was called a
mount; hence, Rydal Mount. It was the lawn, however, that was their treasure.
William praised it in his *Guide to the Lakes*: "This Lawn, a carpet all alive. . . ."
and "This lawn below the house with its crowd of daisies. . . ." They all worked
the soil and experimented with varieties of wild flowers indigenous to the area.

Rydal Mount is now owned by the Wordsworth Trust and is furnished as it
might have been when the Wordsworths lived there. The room to which Dorothy

was confined during her illness was supposedly soundproofed so that her screams and shouts would not disturb the family. At least part of this story is apocryphal, but the guides available at the house don't say which part.

After visiting Rydal Mount, you can return to Grasmere Village along the same path. The views are very different going in this direction; the lakes are constantly in view, as is the River Rothay, which connects Rydal Water to Grasmere Lake. Dorothy describes this area in a 1805 journal entry found in the back of one of the editions of her brother's *Guide to the Lakes*. She and William had set out to walk from Grasmere to Ullswater:

> On a damp and gloomy morning we set forward, William on foot and I upon the pony. . . . As we went along the mists gathered along the valleys, and it even rained all the way to Patterdale; but there was never a drop upon my habit larger than the smallest pearls upon a lady's ring. The trees of the larger island upon Rydale Lake were of some of the most gorgeous colors; the whole island reflected in the water, as I remember once in particular to have seen it with dear Coleridge, when either he or William observed the rocky shore, spotted and streaked with purplish brown heath, and its image in the water, together were like an immense caterpillar, such as, when we were children, we used to call *Woolly Boys*, from their hairy coats.

Figure 2. Rydal Mount. Rydal, Cumbria.

As you approach John's Grove on your return to Dove Cottage, you'll walk along a path that Dorothy frequented and wrote about in her journal; in the area just before where the path becomes a dirt road she would "go backwards and forwards [watching] all colors melting into each other."

To take a different, though longer, route back to Town End, walk down the road past Rydal Hall. This was formerly the home of Lady Fleming, who was the Wordsworths' landlady for a time when they lived at Rydal Mount. Continue past Rydal Chapel, a small church Lady Fleming built in 1824 and where the Wordsworths attended services. Cross the main Ambleside-Grasmere Road (A591) and follow the path to the river. Go through the gate and cross the footbridge over the River Rothay. Continue along the well-worn path through the woods; it emerges from the woods and climbs gently to an open, terraced area above the river. As you continue on this path, you will find yourself a few hundred yards above Rydal Water. You are now on Loughrigg Terrace, located on the side of a flat-top mountain, where Dorothy came to sit among the sheep. She writes:

> I lay upon the steep of Loughrigg my heart dissolved in what I
> saw when I was not startled but re-called from my reverie by a
> noise as of a child paddling without shoes. I looked up and saw
> a lamb close to me. It approached nearer and nearer as if to
> examine me and stood a long time. I did not move. At last it ran
> past me and went bleating along the pathway seeming to be
> seeking its mother.

The views from Loughrigg Terrace are some of the best in the Lake District. From here, both lakes are visible as well as Nab Scar, Loughrigg Fell, and Nab Cottage, where poet Hartley Coleridge, Samuel Taylor Coleridge's son, lived. As you continue your walk, leave the terrace path and follow the path to the River Rothay at the south end of Grasmere Lake. In a shallow section of the river you will see the large stones Dorothy called the "stepping stones." As she noted in her journal: "We came home over the stepping stones the lake was foamy with white waves. I saw a solitary butter flower in the wood. I found it not easy to get over the stepping stones." It is still the same today—if the water is high, it is difficult to get a firm footing on the stones. Cross the main road, the Grasmere-Rydal Road (A591) at White Moss and rejoin the path to Dove Cottage.

WORDSWORTH WALK 2, *The Lake District*

Sites Featured: Elterwater, The Brittania, Skelwith Force, Skelwith Bridge Hotel, and the Ambleside stepping-stones. *Distance*: 8 miles depending upon optional routes. *Degree of Difficulty*: Moderate to difficult. *Time*: Allow a full day. *Starting Point*: Information Center by Grasmere Lake. *See Map.*

From the Information Center take Red Bank Road as it climbs above and away from the lake. The road leads uphill to Loughrigg Tarn, a small placid pond that William called "Diana's Looking Glass" in his poem "Epistle to Sir G. H. Beaumont." Follow Red Bank Road to an even narrower road that goes downhill to Elterwater, a serene valley with a meandering stream and a lake under Langdale Pikes, a mountain range. Dorothy wrote this note about Elterwater in her journal: "When William went fishing in Langdale I sate at the foot of the lake till

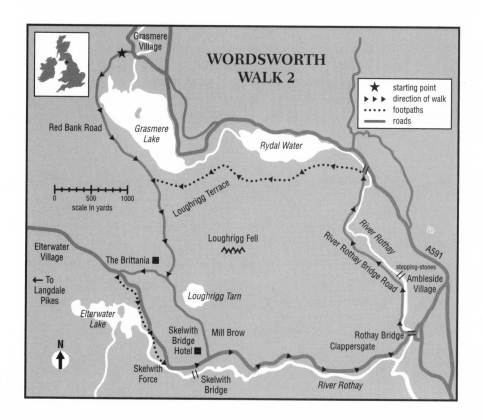

my head ached with cold. The view exquisitely beautiful. . . . The evening grew very pleasant—we [Dorothy and William] sate on the side of the hill looking at Elterwater."

Elterwater's village is at the head of the lake and has a convivial pub and inn, The Brittania. A popular order at midday is their "Plowman's Lunch," an especially good and filling meal. Its digestion requires a nap on the side of the hill overlooking the lake, a site favored by Dorothy. On warm evenings, patrons sit outside and are entertained by Morris dancers, who dress in white pants, white shirts, colorful vests, and hats with many bells sewn onto the costumes; sometimes they also wear animal masks. Their dances are associated with spring fertility rites.

Continue along the path that follows the River Rothay through an open grazing area from which there is a view of Langdale Pikes. Proceed into another wood until you reach Skelwith (pronounced *skeleth*) Force, a waterfall whose torrent is loud enough to drown out all other sounds. The path along the stream and beyond Skelwith Force passes through a working quarry. Beyond the quarry is Skelwith Bridge and the Skelwith Bridge Hotel, a seventeenth-century inn with a restaurant and a pub, The Talbot, which also dates to the seventeenth century.

Figure 3. Stepping-stones across the River Rothay. Ambleside, Cumbria.

This was a walk Dorothy knew well. Here she occasionally encountered poor, sometimes orphaned children from the area. In a journal entry dated 16 June 1800, she wrote:

> [T]he valley all perfumed with the Gale [a myrtle plant] and wild thyme. The woods about the waterfall veined with rich yellow Broom. A succession of delicious views from Skelleth [Skelwith] to Brathay. We met near Skelwith a pretty little boy with a wallet [knapsack] over his shoulder—he came from Hawkshead and was going to late a lock of meal [beg a meal]. He spoke gently and without complaint. When I asked him if he got enough to eat he looked surprized and said 'Nay.' He was seven years old but seemed not more than five.

Just beyond the Skelwith Bridge Hotel is a narrow, steep road that goes up to Mill Brow near Loughrigg Tarn. This is a direct path back to Grasmere. However, the Clappersgate route, which is narrow, winding, and busy, was a favorite of the Wordsworths. To take this route, follow River Rothay Bridge Road at Clappersgate, which goes along the River Rothay under Loughrigg Fell. This is a fairly level route along the river and one that avoids the crowded village of Ambleside. As you proceed along the River Rothay you will see another set of stepping-stones, with which Dorothy was also familiar; these lead to Ambleside. The stones are large and flat, ideal for crossing the water. Dorothy mentions these stones in a journal entry: "Before dinner we set forward to walk intending to return to dinner. But as we had got as far as Rydal, William thought he would go on to Mr. Luff's. We [Dorothy and Mary] accompanied him under Loughrigg and parted near the stepping stones. It was very cold. Mary and I walked quick home."

To return to the Information Center, do not cross the stepping-stones; instead, continue along the River Rothay Bridge Road. The road will end at the bridge over the River Rothay. Rather than taking the bridge, take the path to the left and near a parking area; it follows the river and then later skirts Rydal Water with some excellent views of the water along the way. The path will lead into Loughrigg Terrace. Follow the terrace past the lower end of Grasmere Lake until it bends up to Red Bank Road (you will have to pass through a gate near a farmhouse to get on the road). Red Bank Road leads back to the Information Center.

PRIMARY READINGS

Wordsworth, Dorothy. *The Grasmere Journals*. Edited by Pamela Woof. New York: Oxford University Press, 1993.

———. *The Greens of Grasmere*. Edited by Hilary Clark. Wolverton, England: Clark and Howard Books, 1987.

————. *The Journals of Dorothy Wordsworth*. Edited by Mary Moorman. Oxford: Oxford University Press, 1971. See in particular The Alfoxden Journal, 1798, and The Grasmere Journal, 1800–1803.

Wordsworth, Dorothy, and William Wordsworth. *Home at Grasmere*. Edited by Colette Clark. London: Penguin Classics, 1988.

Wordsworth, William. *Guide to the Lakes*. Edited by E. de Selincourt. Oxford: Oxford University Press, 1970.

————. *Selected Poems*. Edited by John O. Hayden. New York: Penguin Classics, 1994.

2

The Brontës' Moors

*My eye feasted on the outline of swell and sweep—on the
wild colouring communicated to ridge and dell, by moss, by
heath-bell, by flower-sprinkled turf, by brilliant bracken,
and mellow granite crag.*

—CHARLOTTE BRONTË, *Jane Eyre*

To go from the Lake District to the Haworth moors in Yorkshire is to travel from
one extreme to the other. Whereas the Lake District is lush, green, and welcoming,
the moors—a stretch of seemingly endless rolling hills covered in purple heather
and gorse, rock outcroppings, and a few wind-bent trees—are stark, severe, and
foreboding. It is hard to imagine Dorothy's journals or William's poetry being
written in the moors. Similarly, it is impossible to place Emily Brontë's *Wuthering Heights* in Grasmere.

Charlotte (1816–1855) and Emily (1818–1848) Brontë were born to an Irish father,
Patrick, who was the Anglican rector of Haworth Parish Church. Their mother,
Maria Branwell Brontë, was from Cornwall. She died in 1821, within the first year
of the family's move to Haworth, leaving four children. Two other children, both
girls, had already predeceased her. Elizabeth Branwell, Maria's sister, took charge
of the children's upbringing and became the nurturing force behind the blossoming
creativity of the two sisters and their younger sister, Anne (who wrote two lesser-
known novels), as well as of their troubled brother, Branwell. She gave them books
and encouraged their imaginative story writing.

Emily and Charlotte were very different. Emily was introspective, private, mod-
est, and deeply attached to Haworth and the landscape of the moors. She, like
her father, was very fond of Wordsworth's nature poems and the darkly creative
side of Lord Byron. Emily never married and spent most of her life in the
Haworth Parsonage and the surrounding moors. In 1848, at age thirty, she died
of consumption, as tuberculosis was then called. It is rumored that Emily,
though dying, refused to see a doctor or to take repose in her bed, and died on
the sofa in the Haworth Parsonage living room.

Charlotte, in contrast, was outgoing, loved school, and longed to travel and to experience the world away from Haworth. She visited London frequently and became known for championing women's rights. Her social circle included the famous and wealthy, among them William Makepeace Thackeray, the author of *Vanity Fair*. In her late thirties she married the Reverend Arthur Bell Nicholls, who was a curate in her father's parsonage, and lived with him in Haworth. Although she seems to have been something of a reluctant bride, their marriage was a good one for the little time it lasted. She died just a year later in 1855, pregnant and sick with tuberculosis.

Their brother, Branwell, was a talented artist whose masterful portrait of his three sisters now hangs in the National Portrait Gallery in London. His downward spiral paralleled his famous sisters' success. Addicted to alcohol and drugs, particularly opium, he deteriorated rapidly throughout his twenties, accumulating huge debts and spending much of his time at the Haworth pub, the Black Bull, which was close to the Haworth Parsonage. Although Branwell was an embarrassment to his family, his sisters seem to have never abandoned him. Toward the end of his life he suffered from delirium tremens and died in 1848 at the age of thirty-one, without realizing his artistic potential.

As youngsters, Charlotte and Emily, along with Branwell and Anne, created imaginary kingdoms called Angria and Gondal; they developed characters, settings, and plots that became fantastic stories about knights, kings and queens, and heroes and heroines performing great feats of honor. These early stories, referred to as the Brontë Juvenilia, were published long after their deaths. They reveal the sisters' vivid imaginations, later expressed in more mature form in two of the most popular and controversial novels to come out of nineteenth-century England: Emily's *Wuthering Heights* and Charlotte's *Jane Eyre*. Both novels were published in 1847, but only *Jane Eyre* became an instant success.

The sisters published their novels under male pseudonyms partly because of Emily's shyness, but also because they feared their novels would be misunderstood; the strong bias against women writers played a role in their decision as well. Emily chose the name Ellis Bell and Charlotte, Currer Bell (the name Bell probably came from Arthur Bell Nicholls, the curate and later Charlotte's husband). Their apprehensions about how the novels would be received were well-founded. *Wuthering Heights* was seen as a cruel and vicious novel with evil undertones, whose characters were driven by irrationality and excessive passion. It offended many critics who considered it an attack on Victorian sensibilities. *Jane Eyre*, although successful, was attacked by some as being "too masculine," brutal, and coarse.

Haworth Parsonage, where the sisters grew up, looks out on the church and the graveyard on one side; the other side faces the moors. Located just outside their door, the moors formed a definite presence in both Emily and Charlotte's lives. Charlotte, despite her travels, took her vision of Haworth and the moors with

Figure 4. Haworth Parsonage. Haworth Moor, West Yorkshire.

her. She wrote to her sisters and her brother from the Clergy Daughters' School
in Cowan Bridge, some fifty miles from Haworth:

> [T]hat wind, pouring in impetuous current through the air,
> sounding wildly, unremittingly from hour to hour, deepening its
> tone as the night advances, coming not in gusts, but with a
> rapid gathering storm swell—that wind I know is heard at this
> moment far away in the moors of Haworth. Branwell and Emily
> hear it, and as it sweeps over our house, down the churchyard,
> and round the old church, they think perhaps of me. . . .

Of the two sisters, however, it was Emily who was truly wed to the moors.
Even in the harshest weather, she saw in them the wonders of nature's cycle of
birth, death, and regeneration. In her poem "Loud Without the Wind Was
Roaring," she describes them in spring and summer:

> For the moors, for the moors where the short grass
> Like velvet beneath us should lie!
> For the moors, for the moors where each high pass
> Rose sunny against the clear sky.

Emily's great passion for the Haworth moors is perhaps best described by Charlotte. For example, in a prefatory note she wrote for a volume of selected poems

by Emily, Charlotte writes about Emily's experience at the Roe Head School in Mirfield, Yorkshire, some twenty-five miles from Haworth: "Every morning when she woke, the vision of home and the moors rushed on her, and darkened and saddened the day that lay before her." She and Emily had been sent to Roe Head in 1835, and, as had happened when they attended the Clergy Daughters' School, Charlotte adjusted immediately, but Emily did not. In fact, she became quite ill, and was sent home at Charlotte's urging, to be replaced at the school by her sister, Anne.

As a visitor you, too, may discover in yourself a passion for the moors.

BRONTË WALK 1, *Haworth Moor, Yorkshire*

Sites Featured: The Brontë Parsonage, The Black Bull, St. Michael and All Angels Church (Haworth Parish Church), Sladen Beck, Brontë Falls, Brontë Bridge, and Top Withens. *Distance:* 6 miles. *Degree of Difficulty:* Moderate to difficult, depending on weather and ground conditions. *Time:* Approximately 5–6 hours. *Starting Point:* The Brontë Parsonage, Haworth. *See Map.*

The Brontë Parsonage (formerly Haworth Parsonage) in the town of Haworth is now a dark and foreboding museum furnished much as it was when the sisters lived there. One side of the parsonage looks out on the graveyard that connects it to the church; a first glimpse of the moors is had from the rear of the house. The view of the graveyard must have been a constant reminder of death for the sisters. The burial services their father conducted there would have been easily visible from this side of the parsonage. The Black Bull, the pub frequented by Branwell, is located near the entrance to St. Michael and All Angels Church (this is the church where Patrick Brontë was parson) and also serves as a hotel, as it has since the nineteenth century. You can also visit the Sunday school where Charlotte, Anne, and Branwell taught.

After visiting the town and the Brontë sites, follow the path between the churchyard and the church through the gate and onto the moor. The path leads

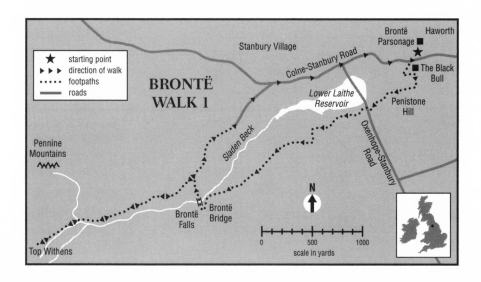

across the Oxenhope-Stanbury Road to the Brontë Falls (it may be quite muddy depending on the recent rainfall). This is a path that the Brontë sisters often took. When Charlotte came home for a visit or when they wanted a short walk on the moors, they went to the stone bridge over the stream, Sladen Beck. The stream has small falls or rapids that are now known as Brontë Falls, and the bridge over the beck is Brontë Bridge. Emily might have been referring to Sladen Beck in this short untitled poem of 1838:

> Awaken on all my dear moorlands
> The wind in its glory and pride!
> O call me from valleys and highlands
> To walk by the hill river's side!

In the middle of Sladen Beck is a stone shaped like a seat. In *Jane Eyre* Charlotte describes a stone-seat in a stream near Lowood School (actually the Clergy Daughters' School at Cowan Bridge), that is obviously the stone in Sladen Beck:

> My favorite seat was a smooth and broad stone, rising white
> and dry from the very middle of the beck, and only to be got at
> by wading through the water; a feat I accomplished barefoot.
> The stone was just broad enough to accommodate, comfortably,
> another girl and me. . . .

The moors slope up gently from the stream, which can be either a soft, rippling flow or a raging torrent, depending on recent rains. Either way Sladen Beck's banks are a good place to pause and sit and read from the Brontës' novels and poems.

Cross Brontë Bridge and go up the slight incline until you reach a fork in the road. Take the path signposted Top Withens. Follow the path through sheep-grazing fields. On the hilltop, slightly to the left, is a lone tree and the remains of a farm destroyed by fire. This is Top Withens, the site believed to be the inspiration for the house Wuthering Heights. The local tourism office has attached a small plaque to the wall, commemorating the site as the ruins of Wuthering Heights. It is a steady climb to the ruin, and it is invariably windy at the top. The trails across the rugged Pennine Mountains stretch out from here.

If ever the interpretation of a novel relied on a particular setting, that novel would be *Wuthering Heights*. It is the story of a passionate, all-consuming love between the wealthy but wild Catherine Earnshaw and the Gypsy orphan, Heathcliff, who is taken in by her father. The two are immediately and powerfully drawn to each other, but are acutely aware of their class difference. When he overhears Cathy make a disparaging remark about his class, Heathcliff leaves to make his fortune. He returns a wealthy man, but Cathy has already married the dependable squire, Edgar Linton. In revenge, Heathcliff seduces and marries Edgar's sister. This leads to everyone's misery. Cathy dies in childbirth, and Heathcliff remains a tragic figure stalking the moors in search of her. After his own death, they are often seen wandering the moors together at night. A little boy catches sight of them and cries: "'They's Heathcliff and a woman, yonder, under t'Nab,' he blubbered, 'un' Aw darnut pass'em.'"

We learn through a character in *Wuthering Heights,* Mr. Lockwood, how the house got its name:

> Wuthering Heights is the name of Mr. Heathcliff's dwelling. 'Wuthering' being a significant provincial adjective, descriptive of the atmospheric tumult to which its station is exposed in stormy weather. . . . [O]ne may guess the power of the north wind blowing over the edge, by the excessive slant of a few stunted firs at the end of the house; and by a range of gaunt thorns all stretching their limbs one way, as if craving alms of the sun.

Figure 5. Brontë Bridge. Haworth Moor, West Yorkshire.

In high winds of the intensity described here, you'll have to huddle beneath a stone wall by the ruins.

Winters on the moors are harsh: the howling north wind bends the stunted trees down to the earth, and water pours from the leaden sky, causing the ground to erupt in fissures. Snow blankets the entire surface and freezes animals in their tracks. When summer finally arrives, its days are as fine as the winter was harsh. The wind calms, the clouds part, and the sun warms the purple heather; above the heath, the birds sing in the clear skies. The beauty of summers on the moors is described in *Wuthering Heights*:

> [T]he pleasantest manner of spending a hot July day was lying
> from morn till evening on a bank of heath in the middle of
> the moors, with the bees humming dreamily about the bloom,
> and the larks singing high up overhead, and the blue sky and
> bright sun shining steadily and cloudlessly.

It is ideal to arrive in early evening, when the last light of day takes on a soft, mauve glow. Sunset on the moors is a spectacular sight, as captured in this passage from Charlotte's *Jane Eyre*:

> Where the sun had gone down in simple state . . . spread a
> solemn purple, burning with the light of red jewels and furnace
> flame at one point, one hill-peak, and extending high and wide,
> soft and still softer, over half heaven.

Local legend has it that at this time of day, Heathcliff's voice can be heard wailing for the ghost of Cathy to come to him, but more likely you will experience the moors as described in Emily's poem, "The Sun Has Set":

> In all the lonely landscape round
> I see no sight and hear no sound,
> Except the wind that far away
> Comes sighing o'er the heathy sea

To return to Haworth you can either retrace your steps or, for a nice loop walk across the moors, you can take a path along the top of the rise, which takes you past the Lower Laithe Reservoir on the north side. To take this path, walk back the same way you came until you reach the fork in the road you encountered on your way to Top Withens. Take the other path—the one you didn't take before—on your left. This path connects with the Colne-Stanbury Road and will bring you back through the village of Stanbury to Haworth.

BRONTË WALK 2, *Haworth Moor, Yorkshire*

Sites Featured: Ponden Hall and Ponden Kirk. *Distance:* 3 miles.
Degree of Difficulty: Moderate. *Time:* 3 hours. *Starting Point:* Ponden
Hall. *See Map.*

Ponden Reservoir was built in the 1870s and is just to the east of the house, Ponden Hall, now a bed-and-breakfast. Erected in 1513, Ponden Hall underwent extensive renovations in 1801. It was the inspiration for the other important house in
Wuthering Heights: Thrushcross Grange. When Emily was a young girl, she came
to this large farmhouse to borrow books from its owner. The Blue Room, now
a bedroom, was then the library. In *Wuthering Heights*, Cathy and Heathcliff catch
sight of the lights at Thrushcross Grange one night as they walk on the moors.
What they see when they peep in through the drawing room window may very
well be a description of what Emily saw there as a young girl: "[I]t was beautiful—a splendid place carpeted with crimson, and crimson-covered chairs and
tables, and a pure white ceiling bordered by gold. . . ."

Follow the well-worn path from Ponden Hall up the slight incline to where
the path forks. Take the fork signposted Ponden Kirk through a gate onto the
moors and follow the yellow arrows along the path. This is Stanbury Moor, a
site that has been designated an area of special scientific interest for its sub-
terraneous reservoirs and streams; development of any kind is prohibited here.
The moor also has a variety of wild life including foxes and grouse. Stay on the
path for about about half a mile until you come to a stream, Ponden Clough
Beck. Across the stream on the right is Ponden Kirk, called "Penistone Crag"
in *Wuthering Heights*. At the base of the crag is a rock with a hole in it. Legend has it that anyone who crawls through the hole will fall in love within the
year. This is the fairy cave Cathy describes to her nurse Nelly during her fatal
illness:

> I see in you, Nelly . . . an aged woman: you have grey hair and
> bent shoulders. This bed is the fairy cave under Penistone Crag,
> and you are gathering elf-bolts to hurt our heifers; pretending,
> while I am near, that they are only locks of wool. . . .

After Cathy's death, a second generation begins to become acquainted with the
moor. Cathy and Edgar's daughter, also named Cathy, is drawn to the "golden
rocks" of "Penistone Crag" much as her mother had been. The path to the crag,
however, passes near Wuthering Heights. Unable to approach the site of so many
painful memories, Edgar must continually draw his daughter away:

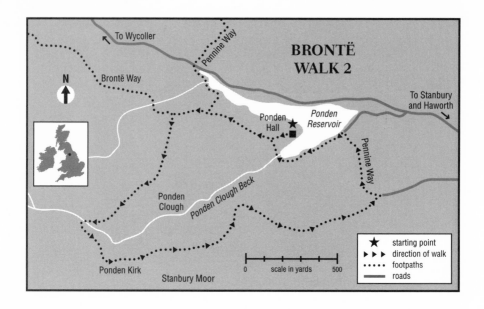

"Now, am I old enough to climb Penistone Crags?" was the constant question in her [Cathy's] mouth. The road thither wound
close by Wuthering Heights. Edgar had not the heart to pass it;
so she received as constantly the answer, "Not yet, love, not yet."

Climbing to the top of Ponden Kirk was a real adventure for the Brontë girls. This climb presents some danger, especially when the rugged rocks are covered with snow. As Emily wrote in *Wuthering Heights*, "[The crags] were bare masses of stone, with hardly enough earth in their clefts to nourish a stunted tree." It is an exhilarating but tricky climb. Once at the top, you will understand why the Brontë girls came here: sweeping views of the moors stretch out in all directions. The view is described in *Wuthering Heights*: "[T]he moors [can be] seen at a distance, broken into cool, dusky dells; close by are great swells of long grass undulating in waves to the breeze." Your walk back to Ponden Hall will take you across another part of Stanbury Moor with undulating hills and dales. Turn left onto Pennine Way for the short walk back to Ponden Hall.

BRONTË WALK 3, *Wycoller Country Park*

Sites Featured: Wycoller Hall and Brontë Way. *Distance*: 3 miles.
Degree of Difficulty: Easy. *Time*: 2 hours. *Starting Point*: Wycoller
Country Park. *See Map*.

Wycoller Country Park is about five miles west of Haworth off the Colne-Stanbury Road. Exit the road at the sign for the park; this road will take you directly
to a parking area.

Jane Eyre by Charlotte Brontë is, like her sister's *Wuthering Heights*, another
tale of tortured love, but it ends with the lovers, Jane Eyre and Mr. Rochester,
happily reunited. Unlike Cathy and Heathcliff, their relationship is of a calmer,
quieter intensity.

Jane Eyre, a quintessential Gothic novel, centers on Jane, a young woman
raised in a brutal orphanage. On leaving the orphanage, Jane becomes a governess for a little French girl at Thornfield Hall, the home of Mr. Rochester, the
French girl's guardian (he once refers to her as "a French dancer's bastard"). He
and Jane fall in love. On their wedding day Jane makes a shocking discovery:
Mr. Rochester's first wife, a madwoman, is alive and lives kept in the attic of Thornfield Hall. Jane flees the house before marrying him. She becomes a schoolteacher
and returns years later to Thornfield, only to find it nearly leveled by a devastating fire set by Mr. Rochester's first wife. She manages to find Mr. Rochester,
who was almost completely blinded by the fire. They marry at last and live together at "Ferndean Manor" (Wycoller Hall).

For Jane, the moors are a source of physical, mental, and emotional support.
They are present in every stage of her relationship with Mr. Rochester. Just before
they first meet Jane is at peace on the moors:

> The ground was hard, the air was still, my road was lonely; . . .
> I was a mile from Thornfield, in a lane noted for wild roses in
> summer, for nuts and blackberries in autumn, and even now
> possessing a few coral treasures in hips and haws, but whose
> best winter delight lay in its utter solitude and leafless repose.

When she leaves him, horrified by the discovery of his wife—"What was I to do?
Where was I to go?"—she heads to the moors for solace of every kind:

> I touched the heath; it was dry, and yet warm with the heat of
> the summer day. . . . Nature seemed to me benign and good; . . . .
> To-night, at least, I would be her guest. . . . I had one morsel of
> bread yet: the remnant of a roll I had bought in a town [I]

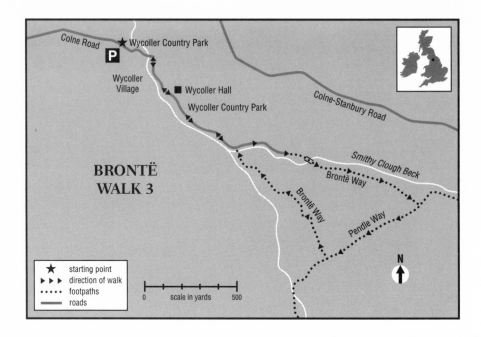

passed through at noon with a stray penny—my last coin. I saw
ripe bilberries gleaming here and there, like jet beads in the
heath: I gathered a handful and ate them with the bread. My
hunger, sharp before, was, if not satisfied, appeased by this her-
mit's meal. I said my evening prayers at its conclusion, and then
chose my couch. Beside the crag, the heath was very deep:
when I lay down my feet were buried in it; rising high on each
side, it left only a narrow space for the night-air to invade. I
folded my shawl double, and spread it over me for a coverlet; a
low mossy swell was my pillow. Thus lodged, I was not, at least
at the commencement of the night, cold.

There are no ruins for Thornfield, but you can visit the inspiration for Mr.
Rochester's "Ferndean Manor." Walk along Colne Road from the parking area
into the village of Wycoller; at the end of the road you will see the gray stone
ruin of Wycoller Hall. It looks like the shell of a cathedral, with its walls standing defiantly against the vegetation that threatens to engulf it. Charlotte describes
Jane's impressions when coming upon "Ferndean Manor" for the first time:

A building of considerable antiquity, moderate size, and no
architectural pretensions, deep buried in a wood. . . . To this
house I came, just ere dark, on an evening marked by the char-
acteristic of sad sky, cold gale, and continued small, penetrating

rain. . . . Iron gates between granite pillars showed me where to enter, and passing through them, I found myself at once in the twilight of close-ranked trees. . . .

There were no flowers, no garden-beds; only a broad gravel-walk girdling a grass-plat, and this set in the heavy frame of the forest. The house presented two pointed gables in front: the windows were latticed and narrow; the front door was narrow too.

Wycoller Hall was nearly destroyed by fire over a hundred years ago, but its former moderate size, narrow windows, and the path to the house are still discernible. Emily might have been thinking of Wycoller Hall when she depicted another building in an untitled poem: "House to which the voice of life shall never more return;/ Chambers roofless, desolate, where weeds and ivy grow."

At the end of the novel, Jane becomes Mr. Rochester's intermediary with nature. Her time away from him and her hours wandering the moors have qualified her to present its glories to him:

Figure 6. The ruins of Wycoller Hall. Wycoller Country Park, Lancashire.

Most of the morning was spent in the open air. I led him out of
the wet and wild wood into some cheerful fields; I described to
him how brilliantly green they were; how the flowers and
hedges looked refreshed; how sparkling blue was the sky. I
sought a seat for him in a hidden and lovely spot: a dry stump
of a tree; nor did I refuse to let him, when seated, place me on
his knee: why should I when both he and I were happier near
than apart? Pilot lay beside us. All was quiet.

To visit Jane's "wet and wild wood," continue past Wycoller Hall, over the small
stone bridge, and follow the path along the Smithy Clough Beck through the
woods. This path is called Brontë Way and follows the stream through these lush
woods. This area is very close to moorland, but the woods are so thick and green,
you would never know it. After a mile or so Brontë Way meets Pendle Way. Turn
right onto Pendle Way and follow it until it loops back to Brontë Way. Go back
along the stream past the Wycoller Hall ruins and on to the village and the parking area.

PRIMARY READINGS

Brontë, Charlotte. *Jane Eyre*. New York: Signet Books, 1997.

Brontë, Emily. *Wuthering Heights*. New York: Bantam Classics, 1983.

Brontë, Charlotte, and Emily Brontë. *Charlotte and Emily Brontë:
The Complete Novels: Jane Eyre, Wuthering Heights, Shirley, Villette,
The Professor*. New York: Grammercy, 1995.

3

D. H. Lawrence's Midlands

A child is born into the world in a special setting and most likely remains inside this setting all his life. He can't get out. . . . A child takes this setting into its consciousness and adjusts itself to it or maybe questions it.

—FRIEDA LAWRENCE, *Frieda Lawrence:*
The Memoirs and Correspondence

"Father a coalminer, scarcely able to read or write—Mother from the bourgeoisie, the cultural element in the house." These were the words D. H. (David Herbert) Lawrence (1885–1930) used to describe his parents in a 1929 article entitled "D. H. Lawrence: Autobiographical Sketch." The family lived in Eastwood, a mining village in Nottinghamshire, England, where Lawrence was born. Though Lawrence traveled extensively and lived for periods of time in Australia, Mexico, Italy, France, and New Mexico, he never freed himself of his Nottinghamshire roots. Frieda, his wife of sixteen years, wrote: "Though he had left his working class, he did not belong to any other, but the simplicity of a working man's way of life was his."

Lawrence met Frieda von Richthofen in March 1912 while he was writing *Sons and Lovers*. Frieda, originally from Germany, was married to Lawrence's French professor in Nottinghamshire. Six weeks after meeting Lawrence, Frieda left her husband and three children and eloped with him to the Continent. They were married in London on 13 July 1914. Brenda Maddox describes their marriage in *D. H. Lawrence: The Story of a Marriage*:

> Theirs was a mismatch made in heaven. Few couples have been so spectacularly unsuited. Frieda, as Mrs. Lawrence, appears to have lacked the wifely virtues of fidelity and a desire to comfort. Lawrence's complete love included throttling her and covering her with bruises. . . . [B]oth were unfaithful in their fashion but

[the marriage] lasted until the end of his life—a life in which he told Frieda, "nothing has mattered but you."

Throughout their marriage, Lawrence and Frieda traveled ceaselessly, in search of political and emotional refuge, as well as of a healthier climate for Lawrence, who had begun to suffer from tuberculosis. Like many in voluntary exile, Lawrence was drawn irresistibly to the memory of home. Three novels clearly tied to Eastwood were written after he left: *The White Peacock*, written mostly in London, was published one month after his mother died in 1911; *Sons and Lovers*, also written mostly in London, was published in 1913; and *Women in Love*, written mostly in Cornwall, was published in 1920. In a letter he wrote from his ranch in New Mexico in 1925 to a friend, Rolf Gardner, Lawrence identifies the corresponding Eastwood settings for each of these novels:

> Whoever stands on Walker Street, Eastwood, will see the whole landscape of *Sons and Lovers* in front of him: Underwood in front, the hills of Derbyshire on the left, the woods and hills of Annesley on the right. The road from Nottingham to Watnall, Moorgreen, up to Underwood and on to Annesley (Byron's Annesley)—gives you all the landscape of *The White Peacock*, Miriam's farm in *Sons and Lovers*, and the home of the Crich family, and Willey Water, in *Women in Love*.

Lawrence evoked these landscapes and the characters that people them with the observant eye of an artist. He was, in fact, an accomplished draftsman and painter. As a young man he enjoyed sketching his family and friends; later, while he was living in New Mexico, he took to painting with the same passion with which he wrote.

After a long struggle with tuberculosis, Lawrence died in Vence, France, in 1930. He had wasted away to eighty-five pounds before dying. Five years later, through the efforts of his friends, his remains were disinterred from the grave in Vence, cremated, and sent off to Frieda in the United States aboard an ocean liner. The urn finally reached her in New Mexico, where she and Lawrence had lived intermittently for years.

Mabel Dodge Luhan, a wealthy woman Lawrence had been involved with (and who had also been his and Frieda's landlady), wanted to scatter his ashes in the desert; she believed this would have been his wish. Not surprisingly, Frieda was opposed. And so, to keep Lawrence's ashes away from Luhan, Frieda had them poured into the wet concrete of the Lawrence Shrine in Lobo, New Mexico.

Who was D. H. Lawrence? Many believed he was a misogynist. In *The Second Sex*, published in 1949, Simone de Beauvoir wrote, "Lawrence believes passionately in the supremacy of the male. The very expression 'phallic marriage', the equivalence he sets up between 'sexual' and 'phallic' constitute sufficient proof."

Some rumored he was a latent homosexual, or at least impotent with women he knew, except for Frieda. Brenda Maddox wrote: "Lawrence was not, like [E. M.] Forster, a suppressed homosexual. . . . Rather, he was a hypersensitive man unable to bring together the male and female components of his personality, and in the grip of a terror of losing the boundaries of self." Perhaps to emphasize, or even defend, his heterosexuality, Lawrence wrote to a female friend in 1912 that he firmly believed in the sanctity of relationships between men and women: "I'll do my life work, sticking up for love between man and woman. . . . I shall always be a priest of love."

Despite the lack of solid evidence, it has also been claimed that Lawrence was a fascist and anti-Semite who supported Germany, and perhaps even spied for that country when he and Frieda lived in Cornwall during World War I. Others take the view that he was a humanitarian, a writer who tried to remain above the politics of his day, even at the cost of his reputation. There is also the possibility that he may simply have been a controversial writer seeking a place to work and the support of sympathetic companions. Rumor and speculation aside, Lawrence's extraordinary talent for bringing Eastwood's landscape to life is universally admired, even by his critics.

The novels whose settings will form the basis of the walks—*The White Peacock*, *Sons and Lovers*, and *Women in Love*—all take place in Eastwood and its environs. *The White Peacock*, Lawrence's first published novel, received mixed reviews, but he was praised for his ability to bring a landscape to life. *Sons and Lovers*, considered his masterpiece by many, is his most admired book and his most directly autobiographical. Lawrence, too, thought it his best. The latest of the three novels, *Women in Love*, was banned for its explicit treatment of sex. Strolling through the settings of these novels is sure to enrich the experience of readers new to Lawrence as well as those already familiar with his work.

LAWRENCE WALK 1, *Eastwood*

The Broxtowe Borough Council and the Nottinghamshire County Council have established in Eastwood the Blue Line Trail, a 2 3/4 mile walk following a blue line painted on the pavement. The walk described here follows the Blue Line Trail. *Sites Featured:* The D. H. Lawrence Birthplace Museum; the Breach ("the Bottoms" in *Sons and Lovers*); the Lawrence family's homes on Victoria Street, Garden Road, Walker Street, and Lynncroft Street; Three Tons Pub ("the Moon and Stars" in *Sons and Lovers*), Congregational Chapel, The British School, and Eastwood Library. *Degree of Difficulty:* Mostly easy. *Time:* 2 hours. *Starting Point:* The D. H. Lawrence Birthplace Museum, 8a Victoria Street. Maps of the Blue Line Trail are available at the museum.

To wander through the streets of Eastwood ("Bestwood" in *Sons and Lovers*) along the Blue Line Trail is to step back in time. Once you move beyond the main street and into the area known as the Breach, you will see that even though the coal mines are gone, the houses built by the mining companies remain and are occupied. There are no towering hills as in the Lake District, nor is there the tempestuous climate of the moors. The landscape here was so long dominated by the coal industry that it seems flattened and dull. Yet it speaks volumes.

Follow the trail from the museum to Princes Street where you'll see row houses known simply as "the Buildings" built by the Colliery Company for its employees between 1830 and 1850, much in the manner of American company towns. Garden Road is another street of row houses that is also part of the Breach, which was a separate neighborhood in Lawrence's time, but which has now become more integrated into town. In *Sons and Lovers*, Lawrence called this part of town "the Bottoms." The name has a double meaning: geographically, it is located in the lowest part of the town, but it also conveys the low social class of the miners who lived there. He describes it as a pleasant neighborhood in some places:

> The houses themselves were substantial and very decent. One could walk all around, seeing little front gardens with auriculas and saxifrage in the shadow of the bottom block, sweet williams and pinks in the sunny top block; seeing neat front windows, little porches, with privet hedges, and dormer windows for the attics.

Soon after Lawrence's birth in 1885, the family moved from 8a Victoria Street to 28 Garden Road, where they lived until 1891. The house, which you can see on the Trail, is featured in *Sons and Lovers*, the story of a powerfully intense relationship between an artist, Paul Morel, and his mother. The novel—considered by many to be Lawrence's most accomplished work—counts among the twentieth century's finest autobiographical novels. Determined that her son escape the grim life of a coal miner, Paul's mother fosters his artistic talent. Their relationship is so profound that it drives away Miriam Leivers, a young woman in love with Paul. In the end, Paul helps his beloved mother die; as she lies suffering with cancer, he gives her a fatal dose of morphine in diluted milk.

Miriam was based on Jessie Chambers, a young woman whom Lawrence grew up with and dated when he was about eighteen. Lawrence's relationship with his mother alienated Jessie, and his depiction of this painful experience in the novel upset Jessie even further. When she read the manuscript of *Sons and Lovers*, she wrote in her book *A Personal Record*: "The shock of *Sons and Lovers* gave the death-blow to our friendship. If I had told Lawrence that I had died before,

Figure 7.
D. H. Lawrence's
birthplace.
8a Victoria Street,
Eastwood,
Nottinghamshire.

I certainly died again." She felt he betrayed her by failing to present a true picture of his relationship with his mother: "He had to present a distorted picture of our association so that the martyr's halo might sit becomingly on his mother's brow." Some of her pain also was surely due to rumors that Lawrence had a crush on her brother, George, who served as the basis for a number of characters in Lawrence's novels as well.

In 1891, the Lawrences moved from the Garden Road house to Walker Street. The Blue Line Trail will take you past the Walker Street house, which is the third one on the street. Although larger than their previous home, its boxy shape and the low wall running around it are confining. It was an upward move for the family, and Lawrence felt that his mother would now at last be treated with the respect she deserved. His parents, however, argued and fought constantly, often keeping Lawrence and his brother awake late into the night. As a young boy, Lawrence would escape the turmoil at home by running off to play in the canyons, the weed-covered, windy field that slopes down the hill to the Breach. Lawrence remembers this neighborhood in a letter to Rolf Gardner in 1926:

> [G]o to Eastwood where I was born, and lived for my first twenty-one years. Go to Walker Street—and stand in front of the third house—and look across at Crich on the left, Underwood in front—High Park woods and Annesley on the right: I lived in that house from the age of 6 to 18, and I know that view better than any in the world. Then walk down the fields to the Breach, and in the corner house facing the stile I lived from 1 to 6.

Lawrence's father, William, continued to drink heavily throughout the years at Walker Street. His alcoholism and the family's domestic problems were partially responsible for their moves, and certainly contributed to his wife's isolation from the community. An educated woman, her cultured background was the cause of even further isolation. A fourth move to 97 Lynncroft, also on the Blue Line Trail, took the family out of the Breach and was Lawrence's last address in Eastwood. In 1908, he left to teach in Croydon; two years later in December 1910, Lawrence returned to Eastwood to be with his mother at her death, one month before the publication of his first novel, *The White Peacock*.

Continue along the Blue Line Trail to the Three Tons Pub, called "the Moon and Stars" in *Sons and Lovers*. This was one of the pubs Lawrence's father frequented, as does Mr. Morel in the book. Just beyond the pub is the Congregational Chapel where his mother attended services. A bit farther along the trail is The British School, where Lawrence worked as a teacher's aide, and the Eastwood Library on Nottingham Road, which maintains an excellent display of Lawrence memorabilia including the headstone from his grave in Vence, France. In the Church Street cemetery a block away is his parents and brother's grave. The headstone reads:

WILLIAM ERNEST LAWRENCE
LYDIA LAWRENCE
ARTHUR LAWRENCE

David Herbert Lawrence, Beloved Son of the Above.
Novelist, Poet, Painter. Born Sept. 11, 1885.
Died at Vence, France March 2, 1930.
"Unconquered"

LAWRENCE WALK 2, *Nottinghamshire,*
three miles north of Eastwood.

Sites Featured: Settings for *The White Peacock, Sons and Lovers,* and *Women in Love. Distance:* About 3 miles. *Degree of Difficulty:* Easy. *Time:* About 2–3 hours. *Starting Point:* Moorgreen Reservoir. *See Map.*

This walk is based on Lawrence's favorite walk in Eastwood, "the country of [his] heart." He describes it in the following excerpt from the same 1926 letter to Rolf Gardner quoted above:

> [G]o til you come to the lodge gate by the reservoir—go through the gate, and up the drive to the next gate, and continue on the footpath just below the drive on the left—on through the wood to Felley Mill farm ["Strelley Mill Farm" in *The White Peacock*]. When you've crossed the brook, turn to the right through Felley Mill gate, and go up the footpath to Annesley. Or, better still, turn to the right, uphill, before you descend to the brook, and go on uphill, up the rough deserted pasture—on past Annesley Kennels—on to Annesley again. That's the country of my heart. From the hills, if you look across at Underwood wood, you'll see a tiny red farm on the edge of the wood. That was Miriam's [Jessie's] farm—where I got my first incentive to write.

His directions are still quite accurate today. However, as he gives the fictional names for real places, they can be somewhat confusing. Also, the growth of neighborhoods and roads has changed parts of the landscape. For example, the path to Annesley is no longer a mere footpath; it is now a paved and heavily transited road. And the Annesley Kennels have long since closed. Nevertheless, the walk Lawrence describes here *can* still be taken. In addition to Felley Farm and Moorgreen Reservoir ("Nethermere" in *The White Peacock* and "Willey Water" in *Women in Love*), the walk features many important sites from Lawrence's novels including Haggs Farm ("Willey Farm" in *Sons and Lovers*), Lamb Close house ("Highclose" in *The White Peacock* and "Shortlands" in *Women in Love*), and High Park Wood ("Spinney Park" in *Sons and Lovers*).

If you are coming from Eastwood, take B6010 out of town to B600. Drive north on B600 for about six miles, and follow the signs for Moorgreen Reservoir and High Park Cottages until you reach a small parking area. The walk from here is through woods and across fields and takes you on a circular path around Moorgreen Reservoir, which is surrounded by rolling hills, farms, and streams. The mines, or what is left of them, are always nearby.

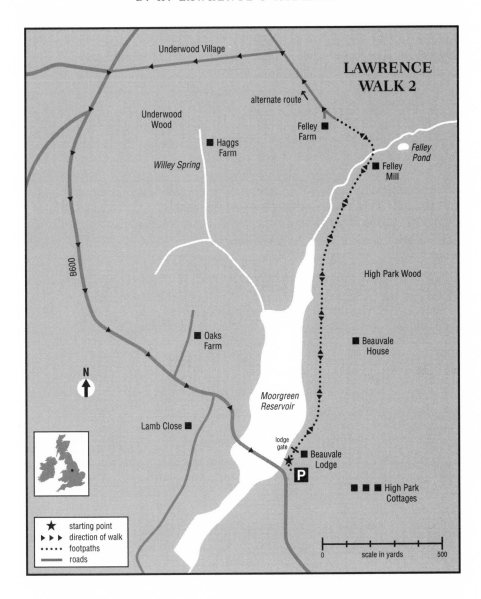

LAWRENCE WALK 2

Underwood Village

alternate route

Underwood Wood

Felley Farm

Willey Spring

Haggs Farm

Felley Pond

Felley Mill

B600

High Park Wood

Oaks Farm

Beauvale House

N

Moorgreen Reservoir

Lamb Close

lodge gate

Beauvale Lodge

P

High Park Cottages

★ starting point
▶ ▶ ▶ direction of walk
• • • • • footpaths
——— roads

0   scale in yards   500

From the parking area there is a path leading to the lodge gate. The path from the lodge gate and on around the reservoir takes you through the world of *The White Peacock*. The novel has a weak narrative that focuses on the narrator, Cyril Mersham, and his relationship with the landscape, particularly "Lake Nethermere" (Moorgreen Reservoir), and the young men of the valley. Cyril relates the story of Lettie who starts out a vain flirt (the white peacock for whom the book is named) and later marries the young squire Leslie Tempest. The novel is not very successful, except for its evocative portrayal of the landscape. Brenda Maddox calls it "absurd and incompetent." E. M. Forster commented in a review:

> There is a passage in *The White Peacock* which is no more than
> a catalogue of the names of flowers yet it brings the glory of
> summer nearer to me than could pages of elaborate poetry.
> That [book] is altogether a remarkable product—so very absurd
> and incompetent as a novel. . . . Yet how vivid the impression it
> leaves!

As you walk around Moorgreen Reservoir, after you've passed Beauvale
Lodge but before you've reached Beauvale House, you'll see a large stone house
called Lamb Close off to the left across the reservoir and B600. It is an
imposing edifice now partially obscured from view by trees and brush. This is
"Highclose" where Lettie and Leslie lived. If you decide later to take the longer
alternate route back to the parking lot, you'll have a second, much closer view
of the house. In *The White Peacock*, Lawrence describes the part of the reservoir visible from the house: "The whole place was gathered in the musing of old
age. The thick-piled trees on the far shore were too dark and sober to dally with
the sun; the weeds stood crowded and motionless. Not even a little wind flick-
ered on the willows of the islets. The water lay softly, intensely still."

This area is also the setting for *Women in Love*, in which much of the action
takes place near Moorgreen Reservoir, called "Willey Water" in this novel. A dark
work that probes psychological and sexual relationships, *Women in Love* uses
the landscape as a metaphor for the sensual. The four main characters, sisters
Gudrun and Ursula Brangwen, Rupert Birkin, and Gerald Crich, establish
meaningful but conflicted relationships driven by passions they often don't understand. Rupert (who most closely represents Lawrence) and Ursula (inspired by
Lawrence's wife, Frieda) form one couple; Gerald and Gudrun form the other
(they were apparently modeled after some former friends of Lawrence—exactly
which friends and how closely they resemble them remains a debated issue to
this day). The mystical yet physical relationship that exists between the two men,
although never consummated, continually undermines their relationships with
Ursula and Gudrun. The friendship between the two couples ends tragically
on a vacation in Switzerland, when Gerald dies on the Alpine ice, leaving
Gudrun alone. Ursula and Rupert marry, but uneasily, partly because of unresolved issues concerning Rupert's sexuality.

The landscape, particularly "Willey Water," is a sexually charged presence
in the novel. Like "Lake Nethermere" in *The White Peacock*, "Willey Water" is
based on Moorgreen Reservoir. Their similarities end here, however. The benign
and peaceful "Lake Nethermere" is transformed in *Women in Love* into a darkly
erotic and dangerous force. It is both the pool in which the self-enamored
Narcissus gazes on his reflection and the water Tantalus is doomed to have just
within his reach and yet not be able to drink:

> One morning the sisters were sketching by the side of Willey
> Water, at the remote end of the lake. Gudrun had waded out to
> a gravelly shoal, and was seated like a Buddhist, staring fixedly

at the water plants that rose succulent from the mud of the low shores. What she could see was mud, soft, oozy, watery mud, and from its festering chill, water-plants rose up, thick and cool and fleshy, very straight and turgid, thrusting out their leaves at right angles, and having dark lurid colours, dark green and blotches of black-purple and bronze. But she could feel their turgid fleshy structure as in a sensuous vision, she knew how they rose out of the mud, she knew how they thrust out from themselves, how they stood stiff and succulent against the air.

The dark aspect of "Willey Water" is sensed physically by Rupert. It teems with life and yet at the same time moves farther and farther along the path to death and corruption. He attempts to explain this to Ursula in a conversation they have beside "Willey Water":

> "Do you smell this little marsh?" he said, sniffing the air. . . .
> "It's rather nice," she said.
> "No," he replied, "alarming."
> "Why alarming?" she laughed.
> "It seethes and seethes, a river of darkness," he said, "putting forth lilies and snakes, and the ignis fatuus, and rolling all the time onward. That's what we never take into count—that it rolls onward."
> "What does?"
> "The other river, the black river. We always consider the silver river of life, rolling on and quickening all the world to a brightness, on and on to heaven, flowing into a bright eternal sea, a heaven of angels thronging. But the other is our real reality—"
> "But what other? I don't see any other," said Ursula.
> "It is your reality, nevertheless," he said; "that dark river of dissolution. You see it rolls in us just as the other rolls—the black river of corruption. And our flowers are of this—our sea-born Aphrodite, all our white phosphorescent flowers of sensuous perfection, all our reality, nowadays."
> "You mean that Aphrodite is really deathly?" asked Ursula.
> "I mean she is the flowering mystery of the death-process, yes," he replied. "When the stream of synthetic creation lapses, we find ourselves part of the inverse process, the blood of destructive creation. Aphrodite is born in the first spasm of universal dissolution—then the snakes and swans and lotus—marsh-flowers—and Gudrun and Gerald—born in the process of destruction creation."

A central event of *Women in Love* is the drowning of Gerald's sister, Diana Crich, and of her would-be rescuer, Dr. Brindell, in "Willey Water" during the Crich's annual public water-party. A life force, "Willey Water" is also a purveyor of death, as Rupert saw.

Even as it takes life, "Willey Water" continues to be the site of life's struggles. In an attempt to rescue his sister, Gerald dives into the black water while Gudrun waits anxiously in a small boat. When he surfaces, unsuccessful, she is driven almost to sexual ecstasy at the sight of him:

> Then he clamored into the boat. Oh, and the beauty of the subjection of his loins, white and dimly luminous as he climbed over the side of the boat, made her want to die, to die. The beauty of his dim and luminous loins, as he climbed into the boat, his back rounded and soft—ah, this was too much for her, too final a vision. She knew it, and it was fatal. The terrible hopelessness of fate, and of beauty, such beauty!

On a moonlit night Moorgreen Reservoir's stillness under the shimmering cloud-filtered light is breathtaking. The water seems so calm; only the occasional fish breaks the surface and the silence. To Lawrence, who saw in the reservoir both the stillness of "Lake Nethermere" and the riot of "Willey Water's" life-and-death struggle, the silence was only a mask for the turmoil just beneath the surface.

Continue north on the path that skirts the reservoir and borders High Park Wood until you are beyond the reservoir. You'll pass the ruins of Felley Mill and also Felley Pond, which is "Mill Pond" in *The White Peacock*. The path becomes a dirt road at this point, and to your left, you'll notice farms. These are the remains of Felley Farm, "Strelley Mill Farm" in *The White Peacock*. Farther across the field to the left is Haggs Farm, the former home of Jessie Chambers and "Willey Farm" in *Sons and Lovers*.

From here, follow the path back the way you came to Moorgreen Reservoir and the parking area. If you are more adventurous, continue on the dirt road past Felley Farm. It will intersect with another dirt road that takes you west around the reservoir and back to B600. Turn left onto the highway and walk south along it for about two miles to get back to the parking area. Although B600 is a fairly busy highway, the road is wooded on both sides and makes for a lovely country walk. From Felley Farm it is about three miles back to the parking area along this alternate route.

PRIMARY READINGS

Lawrence, D. H. *Sons and Lovers*. New York: Barnes and Noble Books, 1996.

——. *The White Peacock*. Oxford: Oxford University Press, 1997.

——. *Women in Love*. New York: The Viking Press, 1969.

4

Lewis Carroll's Oxford

Alice was beginning to get very tired of sitting by her sister on the bank, and of having nothing to do: once or twice she had peeped into the book her sister was reading, but it had no pictures or conversations in it, 'and what is the use of a book,' thought Alice, 'without pictures or conversation?'

—Lewis Carroll,
Alice's Adventures in Wonderland

Charles Lutwidge Dodgson (1832–1898), better known as Lewis Carroll, adored little girls. He was a superb observer, photographer, and artist of them. He frequently dressed them up in costumes and arranged them with toys or other accessories for tableau shots, such as the well-known photograph of Alice Liddell and one of her sisters in ornate silk Chinese costumes. Some have suggested that there was something perverse about his interest in children and have even gone so far as to question his sexual preferences. Although his attraction to children and his preference for their company over that of adults seems odd, no evidence has ever been found to confirm such suspicions. And given the cloistered environment Dodgson lived in on Christ Church's campus, where few secrets could be kept among members of the college, it is unlikely that sexual activity of this nature would have gone unnoticed.

The third of eleven children, Dodgson was born in the parsonage of Daresbury, Cheshire, where his father was a priest. He arrived in Oxford as a Christ Church student in 1851 and remained there the rest of his life, traveling out of Oxford only on rare occasions. At Christ Church he studied mathematics, as his father had, and eventually became a professor there. According to most reports, he was a dull and humorless teacher. Dodgson never married and, it seems, remained celibate his entire life. A terrible stutterer and a poor orator, he shunned the public eye. He did, however, write some highly regarded mathematics treatises.

There is a story, surely apocryphal, that Queen Victoria was so enamored of

Alice's Adventures in Wonderland that she requested that Dodgson's very next book be sent to her. That book happened to be *An Elementary Treatise on Determinants.* A copy is said to have arrived at the palace, but Dodgson vehemently denied having sent it to her.

Despite his rather prosaic-sounding life, Dodgson was clearly inspired by Oxford's enchanting surroundings. The city was a wonderland of marvelous old buildings with bell towers, spires, and gargoyles; narrow lanes and paths through dense gardens and city areas; bustling morning street markets; two swift and beautiful rivers flowing through the city; a university of great renown; and a long and storied history—bordered on all sides by lush green countryside.

In April 1856, Dodgson was photographing Christ Church Cathedral when he saw Alice and her sisters playing in its garden. He wrote in his diary: "The three little girls were in the garden most of the time, and we became excellent friends: we [Dodgson and an unnamed friend] tried to group them in the foreground of the picture, but they were not patient sitters. I mark this day with a stone." Dodgson used this expression in his journals to indicate an exceptional day; not surprisingly, such days tended to revolve around children. With the Liddell girls his stutter disappeared and his wit and humor were awakened. They—Lorina (Ina), the oldest; Alice, the middle child; and Edith, the youngest—were enthralled by the stories he made up for them. Although he enjoyed the company of many children, Alice was by far the most exceptional child Dodgson became friendly with during his adult life. A warm and friendly girl, she was unusually curious, bright, and creative; partly through her influence and presence in Dodgson's life, he developed into one of the most imaginative and beloved English writers of the nineteenth century.

Under the pseudonym Lewis Carroll, Dodgson created *Alice's Adventures in Wonderland* as well as *Through the Looking-Glass and What Alice Found There,* which includes the poem "Jabberwocky," *The Hunting of the Snark, Phantasmagoria,* and countless puzzles, word games, and nonsense word games involving outrageous rhymes and reading backward.

No matter how far-fetched the fantasy world Dodgson created for Alice, stories like *Alice's Adventures in Wonderland* and *Through the Looking-Glass* describe actual places in and around Oxford, and are peopled with characters based on contemporary inhabitants of Oxford. Some of these people Alice knew, such as Professor Bartholemew Price called "the bat," who provided the inspiration for a song sung by the Mad Hatter in *Alice's Adventures in Wonderland*:

> "Twinkle, twinkle little bat!
> How I wonder what you're at!
> Up above the world you fly,
> Like a tea-tray in the sky.
> Twinkle, twinkle—"

Because of this basis in reality and because many of the sites both Dodgson and Alice were familiar with are still in existence and accessible, the admirer of Dodgson's works will be greatly rewarded by a stroll through Oxford. Visitors can even take the same Thames boat ride Dodgson, Alice, and others took during which *Alice's Adventures in Wonderland* was conceived. A walk along the Thames, following Dodgson's boat ride but on shore, is just as enjoyable.

CARROLL WALK 1, *Oxford*

All in the golden afternoon
Full leisurely we glide;
For both our oars, with little skill,
By little arms are plied,
With little hands make vain pretense
Our wanderings to guide.
Ah, cruel Three! In such an hour,
Beneath such dreamy weather,
To beg a tale of breath too weak
To stir the tiniest feather!
Yet what can one poor voice avail
Against three tongues together?

—LEWIS CARROLL, first stanza of
Alice's Adventures in Wonderland

This trip can be taken entirely by boat or by foot along the Thames. **Sites Featured**: Binsey Church, St. Margaret's Well, Port Meadow, Trout Inn, and Wolvercote Common. **Distance**: About 6 miles round trip. **Degree of Difficulty**: Easy, although those not accustomed to rowing may find it strenuous. **Time**: 6 hours. **Starting Point**: Salter Brothers, Ltd., Folly Bridge. **See Map.**

To reach Salter Brothers, Ltd. from Christ Church (founded in 1525 by Cardinal Wolsey), located on St. Aldate's Street, south of Carfax, follow Broad Walk to New Walk, which will take you to the Thames. Turn right at the river and walk to Head of the River Pub and Salter Brothers, Ltd., Folly Bridge. The Liddell-Dodgson party rented a boat from this company on 4 July 1862. While Salter's no longer rents rowboats today, there are other companies that provide this service. Listings are available both at Salter's and the Tourist Information Center on St. Aldate's Street. If you prefer to walk instead, take the riverbank path and follow the same directions given for the boat ride.

Start rowing up river heading northwest; the central part of Oxford should be on your right. You will go around St. Ebbes; through Osney and the Osney Lock; past the Oxford Railway Station and the section known as Jericho, where some of the colleges keep their houseboats and barges; and out through Binsey Green. This stretch of the river flows lazily with wide meadows on either side. You will see a pub, The Perch, off to your left and about 100 yards from

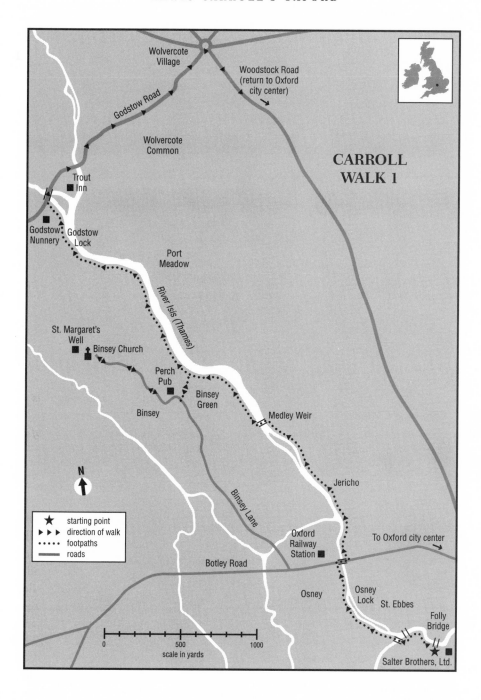

the river. Stop here and secure the boat. Walk northwest along the dirt road just beyond the pub. This road is tree-lined and quiet and curves gently through the meadow where cows and sheep graze.

The road will bring you to Binsey Church, a small and chapel-like structure. Since there is no electricity, it is always candlelit. The floor has a decided slope to it. St. Margaret's Well, sometimes referred to as St. Frideswide's Well, is behind Binsey Church; it has been a place of pilgrimage for hundreds of years. Mavis Batey mentions in *Alice's Adventures in Oxford* that the well had become overgrown in 1857. Dodgson's friend, the Reverend Thomas Prout, cleared it and it became popular once again. Alice often walked here with her governess.

More interestingly, the well appears in *Alice's Adventures in Wonderland*. The reference to it reveals Dodgson's familiarity with the early Christian stories associated with it. For instance, in one medieval legend, St. Frideswide, a princess who became a nun, wanted to establish a convent in Oxford, but King Algar decided he would marry her. As punishment for desiring her, he was struck blind. St. Frideswide so pitied him that she prayed to St. Margaret to restore his sight. St. Margaret answered her prayers by creating the miraculous healing waters in the well now named after her. In the Middle Ages this fluid was known as treacle, now more commonly known as molasses. A popular medieval bible named after this healing treacle was called "The Treacle Bible." The well's history is referred to in *Alice's Adventures in Wonderland,* in "A Mad Tea Party" when the Dormouse tells the following story:

> "Once upon a time there were three little sisters," the Dormouse began in a great hurry; "And their names were Elsie, Lacie, and Tillie; and they lived at the bottom of a well—"
>
> "What did they live on?" said Alice, who always took a great interest in questions of eating and drinking.
>
> "They lived on treacle," said the Dormouse, after thinking a minute or two.
>
> "They couldn't have done that, you know, " Alice gently remarked; "they'd have been ill."
>
> "So they were, " said the Dormouse; "*very* ill."
>
> Alice tried to fancy to herself what such an extraordinary way of living would be like, but it puzzled her too much, so she went on: "But why did they live at the bottom of a well?" . . . .
> The Dormouse again took a moment or two to think about it, and then said, "It was a treacle well."

Return to your boat and continue rowing upriver toward Godstow, through the lock (an enclosed part of the waterway used to adjust the water level), and near the ruined Godstow nunnery. Anywhere you stop in Godstow will take you into the neighborhood where Dodgson, the Reverend Robinson Duckworth, and the Liddells stopped to picnic on their 1862 boat ride. We even have an idea of what they may have eaten from an interview with Alice that appeared in *The New York Times* on 1 May 1932 in an article entitled "The Lewis Carroll that Alice Recalls." Here, she describes a picnic lunch:

[W]hen we went on the river for an afternoon with Mr. Dodgson, which happened at most four or five times every summer term, he always brought out with him a large basket full of cakes, and a kettle, which we used to boil under a haycock, if we could find one. On rarer occasions we went out for the whole day with him, and then we took a larger basket with luncheon—cold chicken and salad and all sorts of good things.

As you walk in Port Meadow, you'll see plenty of evidence of rabbits—rabbit holes and underground burrows. As Duckworth wrote later in his diary, "Nearly all of *Alice's Adventures Under Ground* [later changed to *Alice's Adventures in Wonderland*] was told on that blazing summer afternoon with the heat haze shimmering over the meadows where the party landed to shelter for a while in the shadow cast by the haycocks near Godstow." Dodgson's diary entry for that day reads, "I made an expedition up the river to Godstow with the three Liddells; we had tea on the bank there and did not reach Christ Church until half-past eight." No doubt this is the meadow where that rabbit with a pocketwatch made a mad dash to the hole, luring Alice down after him:

[S]uddenly a White Rabbit with pink eyes ran close by her.
There was nothing so very remarkable in that; nor did Alice think it so very much out of the way to hear the Rabbit say to itself, "Oh dear! Oh dear! I shall be too late!" (when she thought it over afterwards, it occurred to her that she ought to have wondered at this, but at the time it all seemed quite natural); but when the Rabbit actually *took a watch out of its waistcoat-pocket*, and looked at it, and then hurried on, Alice started to her feet, for it flashed across her mind that she had never before seen a rabbit with either a waistcoat-pocket, or a watch to take out of it, and fortunately was just in time to see it pop down a large rabbit-hole under the hedge.
In another moment down went Alice after it, never once considering how in the world she was to get out again.

Row a bit farther up the river to the Trout Inn, which you'll see on the east (or right) side of the river and which is near a spectacular dam. On sunny days it is crowded with students and townspeople sitting out at benches and tables along the river. It is a good place to reinvigorate yourself for the row back to Folly Bridge.

If you walked from Oxford to Godstow instead of rowing there, an alternate route back to Oxford is by way of Wolvercote, which is less than a mile from the Trout Inn. To arrive at Wolvercote, walk northeast along Godstow Road for about one mile into Wolvercote and Wolvercote Common, part of Port Meadow. Wolvercote Common is the largest open space in Oxford, some 350 acres. It is first listed as a common field, or place that commoners can use to graze their animals, in the Domesday Book of A.D. 1086, the census taken by William the Conqueror. In Wolvercote on Godstow Road, catch the bus called The Nipper back into Oxford.

Having retraced the steps of the Dodgson-Liddell party, the last stanzas of the poem that opens *Alice's Adventures in Wonderland* take on added meaning:

> Thus grew the tale of Wonderland:
> Thus slowly, one by one,
> Its quaint events were hammered out—
> and now the tale is done.
> And home we steer, a merry crew,
> Beneath the setting sun.
>
> Alice! A childish story take,
> And with a gentle hand,
> Lay it where Childhood's dreams are twined
> In Memory's mystic band,
> Like pilgrim's wither'd wreath of flowers
> Pluck'd in a far off land.

CARROLL WALK 2, *Oxford*

Sites Featured: The Deanery where Alice lived, Dodgson's home and office, University Church of St. Mary the Virgin, University College, the Botanic Garden, the Deer Park, University Museum, Bodleian Library, the Sheldonian Theatre, Oxford Story, St. Michael's Church at North Gate, and Alice's Shop. *Distance:* 3–4 miles. *Degree of Difficulty:* Easy. *Time:* Allow a full day. *Starting Point:* Christ Church. Maps of the city are available at the Oxford Information Center on St. Aldate's Street.

Oxford is a safe, vibrant, and easy-to-navigate university town. You can take guided city and university walks that start at the Oxford Information Center on St. Aldate's Street, or buy a ticket for the Oxford Tour on a double-decker bus, which provides commentary along the way. Or just follow these directions. Beginning at Christ Church, take the guided tour of the campus grounds and the Cathedral. The guide will point out the Deanery where Alice lived, the right-hand corner of Tom Quad where Dodgson lived, and the library where he had his office and where there is an excellent display of his papers and memorabilia.

From Christ Church take Broad Walk to Merton Grove Walk. Turn left and follow it until it becomes Magpie Lane. Magpie Lane will take you to High Street. Across High Street is the University Church of St. Mary the Virgin. Climb the church tower for a panoramic view of Oxford and the surrounding country. From the church walk east along High Street to University College and enter its gates. This stop has nothing to do with Dodgson, but is not to be missed. Request permission here to view a memorial statue of the English poet Percy Bysshe Shelley, who is depicted resting in a languid pose across the lap of a beautiful muse. It was sculpted in 1894 by Edward Onslow Ford. The following lines from Shelley's poem "Adonais, An Elegy on the Death of John Keats," stanza 55, are fittingly evoked before this statue:

> I am borne darkly, fearfully, afar;
> Whilst, burning through the inmost veil of Heaven,
> The soul of Adonais like a star,
> Beacons from the abode where the Eternal are.

Return to High Street and continue along it, walking past the Examination Schools to the Botanic Garden, a place favored by Dodgson, Alice, and her sisters. It is the oldest botanical garden in England. Once inside the stone walls, you can stroll along the River Cherwell, which is really more stream than a river, and enjoy plants from all over the world. When Dodgson took the Liddell girls here, they often crossed the street to Magdalen (pronounced *maudlin*) College to visit the Deer Park. The Liddell children loved to talk to the deer and asked Dodgson to make up stories about them. If he did, the stories were never committed to paper.

When you leave the park, pass St. Catherine's College to Manor Road, turn left on St. Cross Road, and then right on Holywell Street. Proceed along Holywell Street until you reach Parks Road. Make a right. Go on past Wadham College until you see the University Museum on your right, just past South Parks Road. The University Museum is a striking Victorian building with a display room of iron and glass that vaults up to a high ceiling. It is home to the remains of the last Dodo bird known to have existed. The Dodo makes an appearence in *Alice's Adventures in Wonderland*:

> "What I was going to say, " said the Dodo in an offended
> tone, "was, that the best thing to get us dry would be a Caucus-
> race."
>
> "What *is* a Caucus-race?" said Alice; not that she much
> wanted to know, but the Dodo had paused as if it thought
> somebody should speak, and no one else seemed inclined to say
> anything.
>
> "Why," said the Dodo, "the best way to explain it is to do
> it.". . . However, when they had been running half an hour or
> so, and were quite dry again, the Dodo suddenly called out

*Figure 8. The Sheldonian Theatre in the foreground and the
Bodleian Library behind it. Oxford, Oxfordshire.*

"The race is over!" and they all crowded round it, panting, and asking "But who has won?"

This question the Dodo could not answer without a great deal of thought, and it sat for a long time with one finger pressed upon its forehead (the position in which you usually see Shakespeare, in the pictures of him), while the rest waited in silence. At last the Dodo said, "*Everybody* has won, and all must have prizes."

"But who is to give the prizes?" quite a chorus of voices asked.

"Why, *she,* of course," said the Dodo, pointing to Alice with one finger; and the whole party at once crowded around her, calling out in a confused way, "Prizes! Prizes!"

Return to the Broad Street corner of Christ Church, from where you first set out, the same way you came. Across the street is the famous Bodleian Library, where Dodgson was a familiar figure. Walk through the quad to the Radcliffe Camera (the domed, round building behind Bodleian and a student library), double back through the quad to Broad Street and the Sheldonian Theatre. This trip is part of a loop walk Dodgson took with the Liddells as described in Mavis Batey's *Alice's Adventures in Oxford.*

Farther along Broad Street is the Oxford Story, a building that houses a three-level, theme park-like attraction that presents, in animated form, the history of Oxford and the university, including a brief sketch of Dodgson. Outside the Oxford Story, in the middle of Broad Street, is the marker that shows where the Oxford martyrs were burned at the stake. Turn right on Magdalen Street to the Martyrs' Memorial in St. Giles, across from the Randolph Hotel, erected in 1841 to memorialize the deaths of Archbishop Thomas Cramner, and Bishops Nicholas Ridley and Hugh Latimer. Across the street is the Ashmolean Museum, a favorite museum of the Liddell girls, but too extensive to discuss here except to say that it merits a lengthy visit of its own.

Continue along Magdalen Street heading back toward town; Magdalen Street will become Cornmarket Street and will take you to the ruins of the church of St. Michael at the North Gate. In front of the ruins is a tower from the eleventh century that formed a part of Oxford's original defenses and is the city's oldest building. It was actually moved to the spot it occupies now. As you enter the tower, note the Sheela-na-Gig sculpture in the niche. This kind of sculpture, typically of a woman displaying her genitals and grimacing, dates back perhaps to even pre-Celtic times and can be found in churches and castles in England and Ireland. Many of them have been destroyed, and their original purpose is disputed. On leaving the tower, note the commercial building nearby on the corner of Ship Street and Cornmarket; it is rumored Shakespeare took lodgings here on his journeys from London to Stratford. Some still wonder if he kept one of his muses here, such as the dark lady of the sonnets.

Follow Cornmarket Street to Carfax and into the center of Oxford. This route takes you directly to St. Aldate's Street and Alice's Shop at number 83. Alice used to buy sweets, principally barley sugar, at this shop, and Dodgson used it in the "Wool and Water" chapter of *Through the Looking-Glass*:

> She couldn't make out what had happened at all. Was she in a shop? And was that really—was it really a sheep that was sitting on the other side of the counter? Rub as she would, she could make nothing more of it: she was in a little dark shop, leaning with her elbows on the counter, and opposite to her was an old Sheep, sitting in an armchair knitting, and every now and then leaving off to look at her through a great pair of spectacles.

Walk back up St. Aldate's Street to the Information Center where notices of Oxford events are posted and tickets for them can be purchased.

PRIMARY READINGS

Carroll, Lewis. *Alice's Adventures in Wonderland*. New York: Dover Publications, 1993. Includes the complete 1865 original edition.

———. *The Complete Illustrated Works*. New York: Gramercy, 1995.

5

Thomas Hardy's Dorset

*I'll haunt it night and day
That loveable place,
With its flowers' rich store
That drives night away!*

—THOMAS HARDY,
Concerning This Old House

Read a Thomas Hardy novel or see a movie based on one of them and you will want to go to England's Dorset County, the area he calls "Wessex" in his novels, some 125 miles southwest of London. Hardy lived here almost his entire life. In the space of three miles in Higher Bockhampton, near Dorchester, one can see the cottage where he was born, known as Hardy's Cottage; the Stinsford Churchyard, where his heart is believed to be buried; and Max Gate, the house he designed and lived in for forty-three years.

"Wessex" covers a thirty-by-fifty mile area of west Dorset. During the ninth century, this area was, in fact, called "Wessex"; Hardy simply re-adopted the name in his novels. Those who know Hardy's work will find Dorset very familiar; few writers have set their novels so firmly in an existing landscape. Hardy's characters walk along real roads, pass through real heaths, and visit towns, villages, and even houses that can still be visited today. In his novel *The Mayor of Casterbridge* (1886), the village of "Casterbridge" is really Dorchester, the county seat of Dorset. In *Under the Greenwood Tree* (1872), his village of "Mellstock" is Stinsford. In *Far from the Madding Crowd* (1874), the village he calls "Upper Mellstock" is Higher Bockhampton. The village is crisscrossed by the River Frome and dominated by "Egdon Heath," two prominent settings in his Wessex novels.

Thomas Hardy (1840–1928) was the son of a master stone mason who built and remodeled houses in Dorset. His mother, Jemima Hand, was a cook and a servant maid that came from a poor family; she did, however, have some education and apparently encouraged Hardy's love of books. When he was just eight, she gave him a copy of Samuel Johnson's *Rasselas* and John Dryden's translation of Virgil's works. Hardy, who was the firstborn, had three other siblings about which very little is known.

At sixteen, Hardy was apprenticed to a Dorchester architect for whom his father had worked. He continued his studies throughout his apprenticeship under the guidance of Horace Moule, a classical scholar who became his mentor. Pursuing his career in architecture, Hardy traveled to London in 1862, where he lived for five years, and later to Cornwall, with a three-year stint at home in between. In Cornwall he met Emma Lavinia Gifford, whom he married in 1874. Through her encouragement, Hardy decided to give up architecture and devote himself to his writing. They took up brief residences in several places, until they finally settled at Max Gate in 1885. Hardy and Emma both lived there the rest of their lives, making frequent visits to London and occasional visits abroad.

Hardy designed Max Gate himself and supervised its construction, undertaken by his father and one of his brothers. While living at Max Gate, Hardy entertained royalty, celebrities, and some of the most renowned literary figures of his day, including George Bernard Shaw, William Butler Yeats, Rudyard Kipling, James Barrie, Virginia Woolf, and Robert Louis Stevenson. Another famous and frequent visitor was T. E. Lawrence, better known as Lawrence of Arabia, who lived nearby and was a close friend. Hardy's dog, Wessex, terrorized all who visited him here, including the Prince of Wales. The only one to escape Wessex's wrath was Lawrence. Hardy took this as proof of their deep and trusting friendship.

Despite all the entertaining they did, Hardy and Emma did not welcome unexpected visitors, and both had escape routes to avoid them. She would slip upstairs to her small, third-floor room, and he, with Wessex in tow, would slip into the garden and out through the door in the back wall to the road on the other side. The maid could then truthfully announce, "Mr. Hardy is not at home."

Controversy surrounds Hardy's years at Max Gate, particularly in regard to the nature of his relationship with Emma. Why, for instance, as locals claimed, did Emma sleep in a small antechamber on the third floor, a room more fitting for a servant than the mistress of the house? By 1894, especially around the time he was writing *Jude the Obscure*, it became clear that their relationship was strained. A few years later, Hardy resolved never to write another novel, publishing only poetry and some stories (he published a novel, *The Well-Beloved*, in 1897, but it had been written ten years earlier). Some scholars feel Hardy stopped writing because he did not like the turn his work was starting to take; two of his most successful novels—*Tess of the D'Urbervilles* (1891) and *Jude the Obscure* (1896)—were also two of his darkest, most pessimistic works. Others feel it was guilt over a developing relationship with Florence Emily Dugdale, a woman he and Emma had met in 1904 through a friend, that impeded his ability to write.

In 1912, Emma died suddenly, and in that same year Florence became Hardy's secretary. The beginning of his relationship with Florence is murky, and it is rumored that when the maid came to tell him that Emma was dying, Hardy only instructed her to straighten her uniform. Hardy and Florence were married in 1914.

Of all the rumors and stories about Hardy's life at Max Gate, the most sensational is the one about his heart. As the story goes, when the great writer died at Max Gate in 1928, the locals knew the English people would insist that his remains be laid to rest in the Poets' Corner of Westminster Abbey in London. They also knew that his heart belonged to Dorset. The local butcher was called in. He removed the heart from the corpse, wrapped it in a cloth, and put it in a biscuit tin until a proper burial could be arranged at Stinsford Churchyard a few miles away. Hardy's cat, attracted to the biscuit tin by the smell, got to the heart before it could be buried. Eventually, Hardy's ashes were sent on to Westminster, and his heart (if it survived the cat) was buried at Stinsford in the same grave as the remains of his first wife, Emma. Florence, too, was buried in this grave when she died in 1937.

As Max Gate does not figure in any of Hardy's novels as a literary landscape, I have not included it in the two walks presented in this chapter. It is, however, open to visitors, and I highly recommend a stop here. To visit Max Gate, take route A352, also known as Alington Avenue, into Dorchester from the southeast. Keep a sharp eye out for a small, unremarkable sign for the house, which is on

Figure 9. Max Gate. Dorchester, Dorset.

Alington Avenue a couple of miles from the center of town. (See the additional travel information at the back for further details about visiting hours.) Max Gate, an estate of an acre and a half, is owned by the National Trust, an organization that promotes the preservation of and public access to landmarked buildings and land of natural beauty.

Named for a toll gate formerly located there, Max Gate was built on the site of Neolithic religious grounds that has a stone circle and ritual sites dating to about 2,000 B.C. The Romans later used it as a burial site. Hardy, who appreciated the history of the site, took one of the Neolithic stones, named it the Druid Stone, and had it embedded in the back garden wall, where it still sits today. Hardy writes about the stone in his poem, "Shadow on the Stone": "I went by the Druid stone/That broods in the garden white and lone,/And I stopped and looked at the shifting shadows. . . ." Max Gate is the subject of another poem:

> The house is bleak and cold
> Built so new for me!
> All the winds upon the wold
> Search it through for me. . . .

The house is no longer bleak and cold, as Hardy, perhaps somewhat tongue in cheek, describes it.

Max Gate's garden is a lovely, private Eden dominated by two lawns and a shaded walk along the east wall Hardy called the "Nut Walk" for the hazelnut trees that flank it. In the spring, the entire walk is lined with wild anemones, and Hardy used it both as a place of refuge and as a place to relax with visitors. The Pets' Cemetery, where Wessex and other Max Gate pets (including the curious cat) are buried, is located just within the west wall.

Part of the immense popularity of Hardy's novels is due to their identifiable settings. The correspondence between the real place and fictional place is so close that travelers can walk along the same roads the characters they are reading about did. Readers of Hardy who travel to Dorset and visit the sites Hardy writes about will find themselves transported to the landscapes they had seen only, until then, in their imaginations.

For Hardy sites outside of Dorset, see *The Hardy Guides* by Hermann Lea.

HARDY WALK 1, *Dorset*

Sites Featured: Settings for *Under the Greenwood Tree* and *Far from the Madding Crowd*. **Distance:** About 3–4 miles. **Degree of Difficulty:** Easy to moderate. **Time:** 5–6 hours. **Starting Point:** Stinsford Church and Churchyard. **See Map.**

The sites I have selected from the novels are within five miles of Dorchester. If you are coming from Dorchester take the A35 as if going to Hardy's Cottage and turn off at the sign for Stinsford. Park at Stinsford Church. *Under the Greenwood Tree*, Hardy's first Wessex novel, takes place entirely in the rural locale of Stinsford, Hardy's "Mellstock"; the novel was, in fact, originally titled "The Mellstock Quire."

Under the Greenwood Tree is the love story of the local schoolmistress, Fancy Day, and the squire Tranter Dewy's shy son, Dick Dewy. Although Fancy wishes to marry Dick, her father doesn't think he is worthy of her and makes her accept the proposal of another man, the Vicar Maybold. Dick finally works

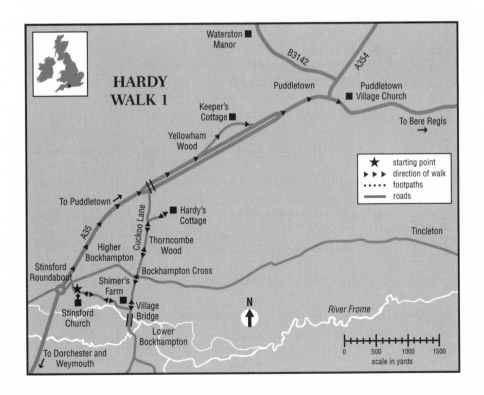

up enough courage to confront Mr. Day with his love for Fancy. The father agrees, and the novel ends in the woods of "Yalbury Hill" (Hardy's name for Yellowham Wood), under a greenwood tree, where a grand, open-air country marriage between Fancy and Dick is celebrated.

From Stinsford Church (also called St. Michael's Church), follow the path eastward along the north fork of the River Frome into Lower Bockhampton. Hardy's "Mellstock" is an amalgam of Stinsford and Lower Bockhampton. This tree-lined path is one that Hardy took many times, and is the same path the string choir in the novel takes for one of its annual Christmas walks. By the time *Under the Greenwood Tree* was published in 1872, the string choir—in which the singers were accompanied by homemade string instruments—was being displaced by barrel organs. Hardy documents the loss of this religious tradition in the novel.

A walk through the villages of Stinsford and Lower Bockhampton is a walk through Hardy's "Lower Mellstock"; many landmarks from Hardy's time are still extant. One example is "Shimer's Farm" in *Under the Greenwood Tree*. To see the home that Hardy based the farm on, continue along the path until it meets a road. To the right is the Village Bridge, which crosses the River Frome. Turn left onto the road, and directly ahead you'll see a private home that overlooks the river. This is "Shimer's Farm." Farther along, you'll see a schoolhouse, now also a private home. Hardy attended school here, and this is where Fancy Day was schoolmistress.

The characters in the novel are intimately tied to the landscape, in this case the woods. It is as alive to them as they are to each other. This close connection is made clear in the novel's opening paragraph:

> To dwellers in a wood almost every species of tree has its voice
> as well as its feature. At the passing of the breeze the fir trees
> sob and moan no less than the rock; the holly whistles as it bat-
> tles with itself; the ash hisses amid its quiverings; the beech
> rustles while its flat boughs rise and fall.

Continue north on the road through the village of Lower Bockhampton. You'll reach a crossroads where the road you are on, known as Cuckoo Lane after this point, crosses a road that runs east-west to Tincleton. This is Bockhampton Cross—Hardy's "Mellstock Cross"—the only crossroads between Stinsford and Higher Bockhampton. *Under the Greenwood Tree* opens here, where various characters pass and meet one another throughout the novel. Continue north on Cuckoo Lane through the village of Higher Bockhampton ("Upper Mellstock" in the novel) until you reach Hardy's Cottage to the east of Cuckoo Lane. The lane leading to the cottage is clearly signposted. The cottage sits serenely in an opening in Thorncombe Wood surrounded by a sheltered garden. Hardy describes this cottage, the home of the fictional squire Tranter Dewy, as "a long, low cottage with a hipped roof of thatch, having dormer windows breaking up into the eaves, a chimney standing in the middle of the ridge and another at each end." The cottage, where Hardy was born 2 June 1840, was built by Hardy's grandfather. Hardy wrote *Under the Greenwood Tree* and *Far from the Madding Crowd* while living here.

The gardens, designed by Hardy himself, are geometrically laid out and planted with humble flowers. The cottage is managed by the National Trust, the same organization that owns Max Gate, and is open during the summer on weekends; at other times it is open by appointment only (see the additional travel information for details). As you enter the tiny, sloping doorway, you'll see "the stone-floored sitting room with the beam bisecting the ceiling" just left of the porch, where the *Under the Greenwood Tree* Christmas party took place:

> Minute after minute glided by, and the party reached the period
> when the ladies' back-hair begins to look forgotten and dissipated;
> when a perceptible dampness makes itself apparent on the
> faces even of delicate girls—a ghastly dew having for some time
> rained from the features of their masculine partners; when
> skirts begin to be torn out of their gathers; when elderly people
> who have stood up to please their juniors, begin to feel sundry
> small tremblings in the regions of the knees.

The kitchen and dining room are to the right as you enter, and the bread oven the Hardy family used still occupies the room. The room at the top of the stairs is the one in which Hardy was born. According to local records, he was thought stillborn until the midwife noticed he was breathing. After viewing the cottage and grounds, return to Stinsford Church along the same roads.

In *Under the Greenwood Tree* Hardy describes the approach to and the interior of Stinsford Church: "At the foot of an incline the church became visible through the north gate or 'church hatch' as it was called. . . . The gallery of Mellstock Church had a status and sentiment of its own." Stinsford Church, where Hardy was baptized, was built mostly in the thirteenth century and restored in the sixteenth and nineteenth centuries. A plaque he designed in honor of the choir, in which some of his relatives sang, can be seen near the tower arch.

In addition to novels with Stinsford settings, Hardy wrote poetry centered on life in Stinsford. One of the most famous of the local poems is "Afternoon Service at Mellstock":

> On afternoons of drowsy calm
> We stood in the panelled pew,
> Singing one-voiced a Tate-and-Brady psalm
> To the tune of "Cambridge New."
>
> We watched the elms, we watched the rooks,
> The clouds upon the breeze.
> Between the whiles of glancing at our books,
> And swaying like the trees.

* * *

Figure 10. Thomas Hardy's Cottage. Higher Bockhampton, Dorset.

So mindless were those outpourings!—
Though I am not aware
That I have gained by subtle thought on things
Since we stood psalming there.

In the churchyard is the simple stone grave that holds Hardy's heart and the remains of his two wives. Next to the grave are the tombs in which Hardy's parents are buried. Also note the grave of poet laureate Cecil Day Lewis (poet laureate 1968–1972).

After visiting the church I suggest making a trip out to Yellowham Wood, an important setting in both *Under the Greenwood Tree* and *Far from the Madding Crowd*. Drive from Stinsford back to the Stinsford roundabout; from here, take A35 northeast going toward Puddletown ("Weatherbury" in *Far from the Madding Crowd*). When you reach Cuckoo Lane, veer left onto the road that parallels the main highway. On your left is Yellowham Wood—Hardy's "Yalbury Hill." There is a small turnoff onto a gravel road that travels through the wood and later rejoins the main highway. There is also an area where you can park and where there are footpaths leading into the wood. Yellowham Wood is the site of the greenwood tree, where Fancy Day and Dick Dewy celebrate their marriage with music, drink, and dancing. Hardy describes the tree as "an ancient tree, horizontally of enormous extent, though having no great pretensions to height." Any number of trees in this wood fit this description.

"Yalbury Hill" also appears in *Far from the Madding Crowd*: "On the turnpike road, between Casterbridge and Weatherbury, and about three miles from the former place, is Yalbury Hill, one of those steep long ascents which pervade the highways of this undulating part of South Wessex. . . ." All the main characters pass through these woods—it is the crossroads of the novel.

Far from the Madding Crowd centers around Bathsheba Everdene, who marries the malicious and abusive Sergeant Troy. The Sergeant "was a man to whom memories were an encumbrance, and anticipations a superfluity. Simply feeling, considering, and caring for what was before his eyes, he was vulnerable to the present." Only after Bathsheba marries him, when she learns that he had seduced, impregnated, and abandoned another woman, does she realize he is a cad. Their marriage ends when the Sergeant fakes his own death by drowning. Bathsheba then promises to marry another suitor, Mr. Boldwood, who kills Sergeant Troy when he reappears. Mr. Boldwood is arrested, and Bathsheba is once again alone. It is only then, after her ordeals with the Sergeant and Mr. Boldwood, that she finds herself attracted to the steady, reliable shepherd Gabriel Oak, whom had long sought her affections and whom she had rebuffed for years. With him, she finds happiness at last.

The first building off A35 heading to Yellowham Wood is a private house, and was once the Keeper's Cottage where thatch was prepared for the village's homes. This is the cottage where Bathsheba took refuge from Gabriel Oak's advances early in the novel. Later, she is sexually attracted to the cocky Sergeant who impresses her with his swordsmanship in a dramatic and dangerous display. She marries him but soon realizes her mistake. Hardy chose "Yalbury Hill" to show us a listless Bathsheba and the dominant Sergeant Troy:

> One Saturday evening in the month of October Bathsheba's
> vehicle was duly creeping up this incline [to Yalbury Hill]. She
> was sitting listlessly in the second seat of the gig, whilst walking
> beside her in a farmer's marketing suit of unusually fashionable
> cut was an erect, well-made young man. Though on foot, he
> held the reins and whip, and occasionally aimed light cuts at the
> horse's ear with the end of the lash, as a recreation. This man
> was her husband, formerly Sergeant Troy, who, having bought
> his discharge with Bathsheba's money, was gradually transform-
> ing himself into a farmer of a spirited and very modern school.

From Yellowham Wood follow A35 into Puddletown, the town Hardy calls "Weatherbury." This is the setting for the second half of the novel. In Puddletown, you'll find Bathsheba's farmhouse on a hill, now a private home called Waterston Manor, and the Puddletown village church. Sergeant Troy sleeps on the porch of the church after visiting the grave of Fanny Robin, the woman he had abandoned before meeting Bathsheba. It is also the church of the famous gargoyle Hardy describes in the novel:

> It [the gargoyle] was too human to be called like a dragon, too impish to be like a man, too animal to be like a fiend, and not enough like a bird to be called a griffin. This horrible stone entity was fashioned as if covered with a wrinkled hide; it had short, erect ears, eyes starting from their sockets, and its fingers and hands were seizing the corners of its mouth, which they thus seemed to pull open to give free passage to the water it vomited.

A gargoyle does adorn the church's exterior wall, but it probably isn't the one Hardy describes here—a much fiercer one than the one you'll see at the church. Hermann Lea, the author of *The Hardy Guides,* claims it was modeled on one from another parish; other sources have suggested the gargoyle from Stinsford Church.

To return to Stinsford Church, take A35 south.

HARDY WALK 2, *Dorset*

Sites Featured: Settings for *The Return of the Native*. *Distance:* 3–5 miles. *Degree of Difficulty:* Easy to moderate. *Time:* 4–5 hours. *Starting Point:* Hardy's Cottage in Higher Bockhampton. *See Map.*

Although Hardy wrote *Under the Greenwood Tree* and *Far from the Madding Crowd* while living in the cottage where he was born, the novel that features its grounds is *The Return of the Native*, written at Max Gate. The loop walk described here includes parts of "Egdon Heath," the Rainbarrow, and other tumuli in the vicinity of Hardy's Cottage.

If you are coming from Dorchester, exit A35 at the Stinsford roundabout and follow the Stinsford-Tincleton Road to Cuckoo Lane. Take Cuckoo Lane north to the signposted turnoff to Hardy's Cottage on the right. Follow the small lane into the parking area; from here there is a short path through a beech tree grove that leads to the cottage.

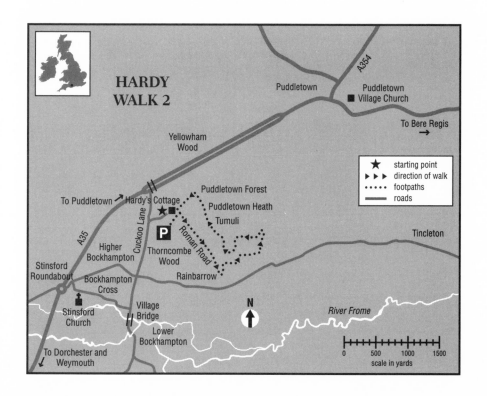

Follow the path opposite the one that leads to the cottage, traveling north-east from the parking area. It leads to what is left of the Roman road that crosses Puddletown Heath (Hardy's "Egdon Heath"), the western edge of the heath. The heath—no longer the vast, open landscape it was in Hardy's day—is now divid-ed, and in some place there are high wire fences closing off military zones.

The Return of the Native opens with a description of "Egdon Heath":

> A Saturday afternoon in November was approaching the
> time of twilight, and the vast tract of unenclosed wild known as
> Egdon Heath embrowned itself moment by moment. Overhead
> the hollow stretch of whitish cloud shutting out the sky was as
> a tent which had the whole heath for its floor.
>
> The heaven being spread with this pallid screen and the
> earth with the darkest vegetation, their meeting line at the hori-
> zon was clearly marked. In such contrast the heath wore the
> appearance of an installment of night which had taken up its
> place before its astronomical hour was come.

In the novel the two main characters, Eustacia Vye and Clym Yeobright, are a young, married, and completely incompatible couple. Eustacia dreams of living in Paris, while Clym, who has just returned from Paris, feels at home on "Egdon Heath." Eustacia's desperation to leave only increases as Clym becomes more and more attached to the heath. She turns to a man with whom she had a pre-vious affair and they run off together, only to drown tragically. The novel ends on the Rainbarrow, with Clym preaching to the local villagers gathered about him.

For Eustacia, the heath is a cruel place she longs to escape: "The heath is a cruel taskmaster to me. . . . " Clym, on the other hand, sees the heath as "most exhilarating, and strengthening, and soothing. I would rather live on these hills than anywhere else in the world." It is indeed a land that provokes strong reac-tions. The heath is also a mystical place because of its traditional associations with the ancient Druids. Like some giant monument to pagan rhythms of life, the heath contains within its borders not just the Rainbarrow, but also the Druidical Stone, and "the Bay of Rainbows, the sombre Sea of Crisis, the Ocean of Storms, the Lake of Dreams, the vast Walled Plains, and the wondrous Ring Mountains. . . ."—all places sacred to pre-Christians. The many nocturnal scenes on the heath, during which the moon is seen in every one of its phases, further defines the heath as a pre-Christian holy place.

Continue on the old Roman road from the parking lot. It will bend toward the south and lead you to a footpath that goes to a small rise in the ground. One of the many tumuli in the area, this mound is believed to be the Rainbarrow, a Neolithic burial site that in Hardy's day commanded a spectacular view of the heath and the valley. This is the symbolic center of *The Return of the Native*; the characters are drawn to it as the moths and fireflies on the heath are drawn to the lights of lanterns and shrub fires. Hardy describes it in the novel on the celebration of Guy Fawkes Day (5 November):

> The first tall flame from the Rainbarrow sprang into the sky, attracting all eyes. . . . It showed up the barrow to be the segment of the globe, as perfect as the day when it was thrown up, even the little ditch remaining from which the earth was dug. Not a plow had ever disturbed a grain of that stubborn soil. . . .

The Rainbarrow represents the demise of an earlier world, but also the continuity of life on the heath. As Hardy says toward the novel's end: "It was at present a place perfectly accordant with man's nature—neither ghastly, hateful, nor ugly; neither commonplace, unmeaning, nor tame; but, like man, slighted and enduring; and withal singularly colossal and mysterious in its swarthy monotony." Although worn down by erosion, it is still impressive.

Follow the Roman road as it bends back up north; you will see more tumuli along the way. You will also see more trees than there were in Hardy's day, as this is now part of a reforested area called Puddletown Forest. The Roman road will take you to a footpath that travels west, back toward Hardy's Cottage. Turn left onto this path to return to the cottage. If you haven't already visited it, I recommend making a stop now. See Hardy Walk 1 for a description of the cottage.

PRIMARY READINGS

Hardy, Thomas. *Far from the Madding Crowd*. The Collected Works of Thomas Hardy, vol. 1. New York: Modern Library, 1994.

———. *Jude the Obscure*. The Collected Works of Thomas Hardy, vol. 2. New York: Modern Library, 1994.

———. *The Mayor of Casterbridge*. The Collected Works of Thomas Hardy, vol. 1. New York: Modern Library, 1994.

———. *The Return of the Native*. The Collected Works of Thomas Hardy, vol. 1. New York: Modern Library, 1994.

———. *Tess of the D'Urbervilles*. The Collected Works of Thomas Hardy, vol. 2. New York: Modern Library, 1994.

———. *The Works of the Thomas Hardy*. Ware, England: The Wordsworth Poetry Library, 1995.

6

Jane Austen's Bath

The first view of Bath in fine weather does not answer my expectations; I think I see more distinctly through rain. The sun was got behind everything, and the appearance of the place from the top of Kingsdown was all vapour, shadow, smoke, and confusion.

—JANE AUSTEN in a letter to
her sister Cassandra, 5 May 1801

The British novelist Jane Austen (1775–1817) is counted among fiction's greatest writers. Some say she is the best novelist of her day; others, that she redefined the novel. The nineteenth-century English critic and essayist George Henry Lewes went so far as to call her the "prose Shakespeare." Edmund Clerihew Bentley, a critic of the late nineteenth and twentieth centuries, perhaps stated it best: "The novels of Jane Austen are the ones to get lost in."

Austen was an extraordinarily private person with a limited social circle. Her forty-two years were spent almost entirely in the company of family and friends, and she never traveled abroad. Much of what is known about her comes from her letters to her older sister, Cassandra, and, of course, her novels. Unfortunately, many of the letters have been lost, as Cassandra destroyed those she considered too personal in nature to release.

Austen, the seventh child of a rector, was born in 1775 at the Steventon Rectory in Steventon, Hampshire. Her family would often read to each other and dramatize stories for each other's amusement. They were very supportive of Austen's work; her father once tried unsuccessfully to find a publisher for an early version of *Pride and Prejudice*, then called "First Impressions."

Although Austen was linked romantically with various men, such as Tom Lefroy, an Irishman who was the nephew of a rector in a neighboring village, she never married. One story from a never-identified family source has her engaged very briefly to a Hampshire man. Apparently she agreed to marry him one day, then decided against it the next. Unlike the character in *Persuasion,* Anne Elliot, who is given a second chance to accept Captain Wentworth's offer of marriage, Austen's suitor died before they could meet again.

Austen and her family moved to Bath in 1801 when her father retired. After her father's death in 1805, Austen stayed temporarily with a succession of relatives and friends in Bath and London. Such instability was upsetting to her, and she didn't write again until 1809, when she settled in Chawton near Alton, Hampshire, with her mother, sister, an aunt, and others. The rural setting of the cottage in Chawton, where she spent the last years of her life, allowed her a quiet existence. She became increasingly reclusive during these years and did little socializing outside the home.

Well aware that writing was not considered an acceptable occupation for women and also for her own privacy, Austen would write at the dining room table after the family had gone to bed. She also took care to hide her activities from their frequent guests. The dining room where she wrote had a squeaky door that would warn her if anyone was about to enter the room; Austen would quickly put her writings away in the table's drawer before she could be discovered.

Austen's novels were published anonymously, and her authorship revealed only after her death. While living at Chawton she wrote four of her best-known novels: *A Novel, by a Lady: Sense and Sensibility* (1811), *Pride and Prejudice* (1813), *Mansfield Park* (1814), and *Emma* (1816). She also wrote and completed *Persuasion* during this time. In May 1817 she was taken to Winchester to be under her doctor's care, and she died there on 18 July, of a then-unnamed ailment that was probably a failure of the adrenal glands, known today as Addison's disease.

Austen is buried in the North Aisle of Winchester Cathedral. Her two novels set in Bath, *Northanger Abbey* and *Persuasion,* were published posthumously in 1818 by her brother, the Reverend Henry Thomas Austen, with a biographical note revealing Austen's identity.

Unlike other writers featured here, who tend to focus on the places in which they were born, Austen wrote about a city she came to know only as an adult, and one that she didn't even like very much. On one occasion in June 1797, after arriving in Bath in the rain, she wrote to Cassandra that her "view of Bath has been just as gloomy as it was last November twelvemonth." Bath was too busy, dirty, and distracting for her, all of which made it difficult for her to write. She preferred genteel country life instead. Nonetheless, she did occasionally write of enjoyable experiences in Bath, and the fact that the city figures prominently in her oeuvre suggests it made a great impact on her.

Northanger Abbey, written around 1798 or 1799 and published posthumously, was Austen's first complete work and also the first in which Bath is the setting. Probably originally entitled "Susan," it was written before Austen moved to Bath. She had visited relatives in the city prior to moving there and wrote the novel in Steventon; she later edited and revised the novel while living in Bath.

Persuasion, written in 1815–1816, just before her death, gives us a view of the city after it had become less fashionable.

Austen's mixed feelings about Bath are revealed in the dialogues and thoughts of the characters in her novels. In *Northanger Abbey,* for instance, Catherine Morland and her suitor Henry Tilney dispute Bath's qualities. Henry warns Catherine of just how tiresome the city can be:

> "Take care, or you will forget to be tired of it at the proper time. You ought to be tired at the end of six weeks."
>
> "I do not think I should be tired, if I were to stay here six months."
>
> "Bath, compared with London, has little variety, and so everybody finds out every year. For six weeks, I allow, Bath is pleasant enough; but beyond that, it is the most tiresome place in the world."

In *Persuasion,* the main character, Anne Elliot, listens to a group of women praising Bath's cheerful qualities during a cab ride. Her own private feelings about Bath, however, are very different: "[Anne] persisted in a very determined, though very silent disinclination for Bath; caught the first dim view of the extensive buildings, smoking in rain, without any wish of seeing them better. . . ." These were very likely Austen's own sentiments.

Despite her conflicted feelings about Bath, Austen's novels make the city an attractive destination for literary travelers. And there is much to see; many of the places Austen frequented still exist and are open to visitors. The walk suggested here will take you to sites from *Persuasion* and *Northanger Abbey,* as well as to sites from Austen's own life.

AUSTEN WALK 1, *Bath*

Sites Featured: Settings for *Northanger Abbey* and *Persuasion*. *Distance:* About 3 miles. *Degree of Difficulty:* Easy to moderate. *Time:* 4–6 hours. *Staring Point:* Jane Austen's former residence at 4 Sydney Place. Maps of Bath are available at the Tourist Information Bureau across from the Pump Room. The Bureau also sells *A Map of Bath in the Time of Jane Austen.*

Bath was a great walking city when Austen's two Bath novels were written, and it remains a great walking city today. There are pedestrian-only shopping lanes, many wide, flat thoroughfares, circles, squares, crescents, and numerous parks and green-belt areas. A bustling city still well-known for its hot springs, Bath is the hub of a fast-growing area in southwest England.

The Romans settled here in A.D. 54, attracted by the hot springs they later turned into baths and spas for their legions. They called this area Aquae Sulis, or the waters of Sul, a local Celtic-Romanized god. The Saxons captured Bath in A.D. 577 and gave it its name, which is derived from the Saxon word, *bathum*.

As noted, Austen had mixed feelings about Bath. She did, however, enjoy walking in the city and its environs. In 1805 she wrote to her sister, Cassandra: "Here is a day for you! Did Bath ever see a finer 8th of April?—It is March and April together, the glare of one and the warmth of the other. We do nothing but walk about."

Begin the walk at 4 Sydney Place, Austen's residence in Bath from 1801 to 1805. The four-storied, terraced apartment building is located across the River Avon via Pulteney Bridge and Great Pulteney Street. When Austen moved here, Sydney Place was at the edge of Bath and overlooked fields and outlying houses. Now it is surrounded by houses and apartment buildings.

Austen loved gardens, and she often frequented Bath's Sydney Gardens located just across from Sydney Place at the end of Great Pulteney Street. Laid out in 1795 behind the Holburne Art Museum, the gardens are beautifully maintained and boast tree-shaded paths and a hedge maze. While house hunting in Bath in 1801, Austen wrote to Cassandra: "It would be very pleasant to be near Sydney Gardens! We might go into the labyrinth [the hedge maze] every day."

Walk back toward the center of the city along Great Pulteney Street, a large, broad street lined with gray-white Palladian-style buildings. This street is the residence of Catherine Morland in *Northanger Abbey* (completed in 1803 but not published until late 1817). Catherine, a young woman from a small country village, arrives in Bath for a six-week stay. Immediately upon her arrival, she is introduced to the life of a young woman of privilege. The Allens, her guardians, take

Figure 11. Jane Austen's residence in Bath. 4 Sydney Place, Bath, Avon.

up "comfortable lodgings in Pulteney Street" and Mrs. Allen, of whom it is said that "[d]ress is her passion," soon sees to it that Catherine is fashionably dressed. Catherine, however, is more interested in people than clothes and takes pleasure in being introduced to Bath society. At a dance she meets Henry Tilney, a country clergyman, and they fall in love. Although Henry's father, a general, disapproves of the match, Henry seeks her out at her home and they marry at Northanger Abbey, about a day's journey by carriage from Bath.

Great Pulteney Street leads directly to Pulteney Bridge. Austen went this way whenever she walked to the Assembly Rooms or the Pump Room, two sites that will be visited farther along. Pulteney Bridge is small, narrow, and crammed with shops, rather like a miniature version of the Ponte Vecchio in Florence, Italy. After crossing the bridge, turn left to follow the river walk. You'll pass the large dam where local youths cool off on hot summer days, and the Parade Gardens, which feature seasonal flowers—daffodils in spring, roses in summer.

The Lower Assembly Rooms, which are no longer extant, were located near the Parade Gardens. Like the Upper Assembly Rooms (described below), the Lower Rooms were places for social gatherings in Austen's time. This is where Catherine first meets and dances with Henry. Young, fashionable men and women gathered here night and day to see and be seen, as well as to dine, dance, and drink tea or champagne. Mrs. Allen, who accompanies Catherine to the

Assembly Rooms the night she meets Henry, is thankful that she "preserved her gown from injury" in the crush of people.

As you leave the Parade Gardens, turn right at North Parade, a pedestrian-only street, and continue into the heart of the city. On your right you'll find Sally Lunn's, a tea shop that claims to be the oldest inhabited building in Bath. Stop in for a Bath Bun (something like a doughy hot cross bun) and tea. Austen, in a letter to Cassandra, complains about "disordering her stomach with Bath Bunns." I have had many Bath Buns over the years and never has my stomach been disordered. Follow North Parade Street into the Abbey Churchyard, formerly called the Pump Yard. You are now in the heart of Bath, in the churchyard enclosed by three streets: York, Stall, and Cheap, named for the outdoor markets once held here where one could bargain for food and goods. As you stand in the Abbey Churchyard with the Abbey behind you, the Pump Room and Roman Baths are to your left and the Tourist Information Bureau to your right.

The Pump Room was another of the social centers in Austen's day. One can still eat, have tea, and meet friends here. It is called the Pump Room because water from the Roman Baths used to be pumped up here. The building contains a concert hall, reading rooms, a terrace restaurant overlooking a Roman Bath, and the Pump Room itself where water is still pumped in. You can taste the water, which has a sulfuric smell and bitter taste, and see the Roman plumbing through which the hot water is brought in, in the building's basement.

Many key events in *Northanger Abbey* occur at the Pump Room. Just outside, in the Pump Yard, Catherine and her friend Isabella start out on a walk and have trouble crossing busy Cheap Street: "Half a minute conducted them through the Pump-yard to the archway, opposite Union Passage. . . . Everybody acquainted with Bath may remember the difficulties of crossing Cheap Street at this point. . . ." Before she meets Henry and John Thorpe, Isabella's brother, Catherine's routine in Bath is circumscribed by the Pump Room, the Upper and Lower Halls, the theater, the church, and walks in the Crescent: "Every morning now brought its regular duties; shops were to be visited, some new part of the town to be looked at, and the Pump Room to be attended, where they paraded up and down for an hour, looking at everybody and speaking to no one." With the women she meets, she discusses "dress, balls, flirtations, and quizzes." Other activities include attending the theater, going to church on Sunday, and after church, weather permitting, taking walks in the fashionable parts of town.

Persuasion, written twenty years later, takes place in the period following the Napoleonic Wars. Austen demonstrates the wars' impact on the lives of her characters as well as on the city itself, which she portrays as markedly less fashionable and overrun by commoners. The heroine, Anne Elliot, is twenty-seven years old and unmarried—practically an old maid by the standards of her day. At twenty she had turned down a marriage proposal from Captain Wentworth because her father disapproved of the match. She regrets the lost opportunity but is resigned to it. A second opportunity presents itself when she and Captain

Wentworth meet again in Bath, and this time Anne does not hesitate to accept his proposal.

From the Pump Room, walk north along the colonnaded Bath Street to the Abbey Church House built in the sixteenth century (it is the gabled-roof building near the Technical College), which in Austen's day was called Hetling House. It once had a pump to bring "healing waters" up from the hot springs below. This area of Bath had numerous "Spa Houses" in which the waters were used to treat everything from gout to rheumatism.

Continue north along Bath Street until you reach the Westgate Buildings, a long line of substantial stone structures. In *Persuasion*, Mrs. Smith, an old schoolmate of Anne's, lives here to take advantage of the waters from a nearby spa. Anne's father, Sir Walter, criticizes her for being seen at the Westgate Buildings, which were in what was then the poorer section of town. When Anne visits Mrs. Smith, now a poor widow crippled with arthritis, Sir Walter's reaction is cruel and unfeeling:

> "A widow Mrs. Smith lodging in Westgate Buildings! A poor
> widow, barely able to live, between thirty and forty; a mere Mrs.
> Smith, an every-day Mrs. Smith, of all people and all names in
> the world, to be the chosen friend of Miss Anne Elliot, and to
> be preferred by her to her own family connections among the
> nobility of England and Ireland!"

From the Westgate Buildings, continue north on Bath Street to Barton Street and Beaufort Square. Here, you'll see the Theatre Royal, which opened in 1805, as well as the residence of Richard Nash (also known as Beau Nash), an eighteenth-century dandy and social arbiter known about town as the "King of Bath" (he died in this house in 1762). Turn right at Wood Street and follow it until it becomes Quiet Street (no longer free from noise and strife) to Milsom Street. This is a wonderful shopping area, little changed from Austen's time. The Octagon, an eight-sided building erected as a chapel in 1767 and now home to the Royal Photographic Society, is found here along with numerous antique shops, restaurants, and pubs. It was on Milsom Street that Anne saw Admiral Croft, whom she knew to be a friend of Captain Wentworth's, looking in the window of a print shop: "He was standing by himself, at a printshop window, with his hands behind him, in earnest contemplation of some print, and she not only might have passed him unseen, but was obliged to touch as well as address him before she could get his notice."

After she gets his attention, Anne and the admiral take a walk together. The admiral informs Anne that Captain Wentworth is once again available and coming to Bath. Louisa Musgrove, the captain's fiancée, has chosen someone else. The admiral says, "Poor Frederick! . . . Now he must begin all over again with somebody else. I think we must get him to Bath. . . . Do you not think, Miss Elliot, we had better try to get him to Bath?" She readily acquiesces.

At the top of Milsom Street, turn right on George Street and then almost immediately left on Bartlett Street. Continue along Bartlett Street until you reach Alfred Street. Turn right here. Take Alfred Street to Lansdown Road and then turn left. Lansdown will take you to Camden Crescent. This part of the walk is steep, and Anne calls it a "toilsome walk." The Elliots in *Persuasion* lived in Camden Crescent, then called Camden Place. It is on a walk from Union Street to Camden Crescent that Captain Wentworth and Anne are finally reconciled:

> There they returned again into the past, more exquisitely
> happy, perhaps, in their reunion, than when it had been first
> projected; more tender, more tried, more fixed in a knowledge
> of each other's character, truth and attachment, more equal
> to act, more justified in acting.

Return to Lansdown Road. Turn right here and walk until you reach Morford Street; make a left. Continue until you encounter Russell Street and then make a right. Go on from there to the top of Alfred Street and the Costume Museum. In Austen's day, this building was known as the Upper Assembly Rooms to contrast it from the Lower Assembly Rooms. Austen visited the Upper Rooms to dance, have tea, and meet friends and relations. This was another socially approved place to mingle with the opposite sex. In *Northanger Abbey,* Catherine wasn't permitted to go to the Upper Rooms until Mrs. Allen was convinced that Catherine was "presentable." It is here that she makes her social debut:

> Her hair was cut and dressed by the best hand, her clothes put
> on with care, and both Mrs. Allen and her maid declared she
> looked quite as she should do. . . . The season was full, the
> room crowded, and the two ladies squeezed in as well as they
> could. . . . [T]hough by unwearied diligence they gained even
> the top of the room, their situation was just the same; they saw
> nothing of the dancers but the high feathers of some ladies.

This part of town, known as the upper town, dates back to the eighteenth century. The architecture is splendidly Georgian, and the streets are broad and tree-lined. Continue on Alfred Street to the Circus, a circle of Neoclassical buildings around a park. Formerly called the King's Circus, the Circus was designed by John Wood the Elder in 1754 and completed by his son John Wood the Younger in 1758.

From the Circus take Brock Street to the Royal Crescent, an ellipse-shaped apartment building 600 feet in length. Designed by John Wood the Younger, the thirty large Georgian-style apartments feature 114 huge Ionic columns. Apartment 1 is open to the public and is a fine example of a Georgian Terrace House as described in Austen's novels. Maintained by the Bath Preservation Trust, it is fully restored and furnished in eighteenth-century style. This area was another popular place to go walking in Austen's time. Catherine and her friends mention taking walks here: "They hastened away to the Crescent to breathe the fresh air."

Just beyond the Royal Crescent is Royal Victoria Park and the High Common leading to Sion Hill. The path up Sion Hill is steep but rewards those who exert themselves with superb views of the city. It was one of Austen's more strenuous walks. In a letter she wrote to Cassandra in 1801 she says: "We went up by Sion Hill and returned across the fields."A loop walk through Victoria Park, to Sion Hill, and back to the Royal Crescent, all along the same path makes for an enjoyable trek. To return to the town, take Gay Street south from the Royal Crescent. Austen lived briefly on this street after her father's death, and in *Persuasion*, the now married Admiral Croft and his wife take lodgings on this street. From Gay Street, it's a short walk back into the center of town.

PRIMARY READINGS

Austen, Jane. *Emma*. The Complete Novels of Jane Austen, vol. 2. New York: Modern Library, 1996.

———. *Mansfield Park*. The Complete Novels of Jane Austen, vol. 1. New York: Modern Library, 1996.

———. *Northanger Abbey*. The Complete Novels of Jane Austen, vol. 2. Modern Library, 1996.

———. *Persuasion*. The Complete Novels of Jane Austen, vol. 2. Modern Library, 1996.

———. *Pride and Prejudice*. The Complete Novels of Jane Austen, vol. 1. New York: Modern Library, 1996.

———. *Sense and Sensibility*. The Complete Novels of Jane Austen, vol. 1. New York: Modern Library, 1996.

7

Dylan Thomas's Wales

I was born in a large Welsh industrial town (Swansea) at the beginning of the Great War: an ugly, lovely town (or so it was, and is, to me), crawling, sprawling, slummed, unplanned, jerry-villa'd, and smug-suburbed by the side of a long and splendid-curving shore where truant boys and sandfield boys and old anonymous men, in the tatters and hangovers of a hundred charity suits, beachcombed, idled, and paddled, watched the dock-bound boats, threw stones into the sea for the barking, outcast dogs, and, on Saturday summer afternoons, listened to the militant music of salvation and hell-fire preached from a soap-box.

—DYLAN THOMAS, "Reminiscences of Childhood"
in *Quite Early One Morning*

Nothing less than the sound of Wales is what one hears in the poetry and prose of Dylan Thomas (1914–1953). His is the cadence of Wales. With images ranging from the Welsh city, Swansea, to the villages, Laugharne and Llangain, he chronicles the life of the Welsh man from childhood to adulthood, from innocence to experience, the way no one else has. Thomas defines Wales the way James Joyce defines Ireland—in language and myth.

The tradition of poetry as a central part of the culture is stronger in Wales and Ireland than in the rest of the British Isles. Both countries have legendary poets who were considered shamans and prophets for their exceptional use of language. One word from them could transform—even kill—the object of their barbs. Poets were not to be trifled with and were accorded royal status at gatherings of the early Welsh Celtic tribes.

Important to Welsh literature are the medieval poems and tales of the

*Figure 12. Dylan Thomas's birthplace. 5 Cwmdonkin Drive,
The Uplands in Swansea, West Glamorgan, Wales.*

Mabinogi, a set of mythical stories full of heroic feats, strange beasts, and beautiful maidens, much in the tradition of the legends of the Irish-Celtic hero
Cuchulain (pronounced *cuhoolin*). The writings of the *Mabinogi* can be
traced back much further than the medieval era; their roots are found in the
earliest stories of the Welsh people. Thomas's first name, chosen by his
father, was taken from the *Mabinogi*: "And Math son of Mathonwy said: 'I shall
name this child, and the name I shall give him is Dylan.'" The name means
Sea Son of the Wave.

Although Thomas doesn't refer directly to these early Welsh works, an atten-
tive reader will find that he is a poet in the truest sense of these mythic begin-

nings, which are very different from the English poetic tradition. For example, Matthew Arnold (1822–1888), the English poet and essayist, in his *On the Study of Celtic Literature* (1867), quotes this passage from the *Mabinogi*: "And they saw a tall tree by the side of the river, one half of which was in flames from the root to the top, and the other half was green and in full leaf." Arnold claims no Englishman could have written that passage and its pattern of imagery. Constantine Fitzgibbon in *The Life of Dylan Thomas* (1965) agrees with Arnold and adds, "Dylan [Thomas] on the other hand, could and did write in this way."

Thomas was born on 27 October 1914 at 5 Cwmdonkin Drive in The Uplands, a local name for this area of Swansea, Wales. His father was English master at Swansea Grammar School and a stern taskmaster. His mother, though born in Swansea, was brought up on a farm in Llangain, some twenty miles northwest of Swansea. He had one sister, eight years older. At the age of ten, Thomas began attending Swansea Grammar School, where his father was English master, and at twenty, moved to London.

Thomas loved his mother, but he both loved and feared his father. He and his father did, however, grow quite close eventually, though late in his father's life. Thomas was deeply shaken by his father's agonizing death brought on by complications from tongue cancer. One of his most famous poems, "Do Not Go Gentle into That Good Night," was written as a tribute to him.

Thomas tried to sell his poetry, but met at first with more rejections than acceptances. Nevertheless, he continued to write and worked as a journalist and, on occasion, as an actor. During this period, he divided his time between London and 5 Cwmdonkin Drive. His *Eighteen Poems* (1934) and later, *Twenty-five Poems* (1936), were his first successes, although controversial.

One night in a London pub, he was introduced to Caitlin Macnamara. Theirs was an immediate and passionate affair. They married in Penzance, Cornwall, in 1937 and settled the next year in Laugharne, a Welsh fishing village. For the rest of their lives together, they shared an intense, tempestuous relationship that often resulted in physical brawls, no doubt owing, at least in part, to their prodigious consumption of alcohol and their mutual infidelity. Fitzgibbon writes that Thomas once told friends in New York: "It doesn't matter who I go to bed with, because they're all really Caitlin."

Stories of their life together are legendary. Supposedly, Caitlin would sometimes wait on the path to their cottage for the drunken Thomas to return home after a pub crawl. Armed with chinaware, she would begin hurling dishes and epithets at him in equal proportions as he staggered up the path. Her fiery Irish temper clashed with his Welsh resolve, and their marriage was often threatened by their unwillingness to compromise.

During World War II Thomas continued to divide his time between England and Wales. Immediately after the war, from 1945 to 1949, he spent time at Oxford and traveled to Italy, Ireland, and Czechoslovakia, occasionally taking Caitlin, but usually going alone. He thought seriously of emigrating to the United

States where he was awarded the Levinson Prize for poetry in Chicago in 1945. But as he wrote in his poem titled "I Have Longed to Move Away," "I have longed to move away but am afraid." Laugharne remained his home, and this was where his three children were brought up.

Thomas led the life of a reckless bohemian poet, drinking to excesses hard to imagine, smoking, and generally disobeying doctors' advice. He had financial problems all his life and knew little peace except when writing poetry in his shed near his cottage, known as the Boat House, in Laugharne. In his short life he produced a burst of poetry that took the English-speaking world—particularly America—by storm. He made four immensely successful, if short, lecture trips to the United States in the early 1950s, attracting an emotional, dedicated, and cultlike following from Chicago to New York. It was his poetry that inspired such devotion, but it was also his brilliant reading performances. The recordings of his readings are well worth listening to, and many that have seen and heard Thomas read in person consider it an incomparable experience.

Thomas died in New York City on 9 November 1953 at age thirty-nine during the last of his aforementioned lecture trips. Just before his death, he was working on *Under Milk Wood*, a radio play, and giving poetry readings at the Poetry Center in New York. He was also taking pep pills and receiving doctor-administered cortisone injections to help relieve stress and restore him from a state of near collapse. He continued to drink, however, and finally did collapse after drinking an enormous quantity of whiskey (some say he had as many as seventeen shots) at The White Horse Tavern in New York's West Village, a still-extant pub that has a room dedicated to him. He was taken to St. Vincent's Hospital in a coma and soon contracted pneumonia. This was listed as the cause of death, although one doctor diagnosed it as an "insult to the brain" brought on by alcohol.

Thomas's hold on Caitlin remained strong after his death, although she later remarried. With her second husband, Giuseppe Fazio, a Sicilian movie director, she lived a more conventional life. She writes in her memoir, *Leftover Life to Kill*:

> [Thomas] said he loved me; that I was the only woman for him; and, whatever the evidence to the contrary, I believed him, and still do; and I am grateful for that important bit of faith. There is, happily, no limit to the faith of human nature in believing what it wants to believe. But the sudden removal of such a love, such a special love, on such an immortal scale, and the only one, was bound to cause a dropping out of the bottom of my all-in-Dylan world.

Caitlin died in Catania, Sicily, in 1994 and was buried at Thomas's side in the church graveyard in Laugharne.

For his admirers, one of the most poignant ways of remembering Thomas is through his poem "Fern Hill," which captures the fleeting beauty of youth. This poem commemorates the happy moments Thomas spent as a child at the farm of his aunt Ann Jones outside Llangain, near Carmarthen, Wales:

> Now as I was young and easy under the apple boughs
> About the lilting house and happy as the grass was green,
>   The night above the dingle starry,
>   Time let me hail and climb
>   Golden in the heydays of his eyes,
> And honored among wagons I was prince of the apple towns

THOMAS WALK 1, *The Uplands of Swansea, Wales*

Sites Featured: Uplands Crescent, The Uplands Hotel, Mrs. Holt's dame school, the Grove, Thomas's birthplace, and Cwmdonkin Park. *Distance:* 3–5 miles, depending on side trips and park excursions. *Degree of Difficulty:* Moderate. *Time:* Half day. *Starting Point:* Uplands Crescent. *See Map.*

The Uplands, one of the oldest residential areas in Swansea, has narrow streets that often end in cul-de-sacs. Uplands Crescent, formerly High Street, Gwyder Square, is the center of the small but active Uplands shopping area. Most of the shops Thomas knew as a boy are gone and replaced by new ones, but the essential flavor of the area has probably changed little. One place still in existence from his childhood days is The Uplands Hotel, located right on Uplands Crescent. In "Return Journey" (included in *A Dylan Thomas Treasury*), a story he wrote for a BBC broadcast, he wrote: "I went out of the hotel into the snow and walked down High Street, past the flat white wastes where all the shops had been." His favorite place, however, the cinema, is gone, and a bank stands in its place. Thomas, who was very fond of American cowboy movies, wrote in "Return Journey," "Here was once the flea-pit picture house where he [Thomas as a boy] whooped for the scalping Indians . . . and banged for the rustler's guns." Often,

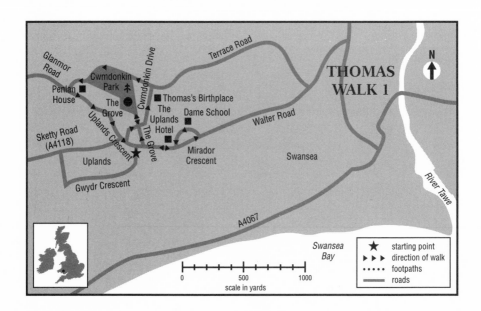

on his way back home from the cinema, this part of Swansea, with its alleys and unlit lanes behind the shops, would become the American West for a group of Welsh youngsters.

Walk east until Uplands Crescent becomes Walter Road; continue on the road to the corner of Mirador Crescent. Turn left on Mirador Crescent. Thomas attended Mrs. Holt's dame school (a school taught by a woman) in a private house on this street before he entered Swansea Grammar School. In *Reminiscences of Childhood* (1943), he wrote: "So I remember that never was there such a dame-school as ours. . . . Behind the school was a narrow lane where the oldest and boldest threw pebbles at windows, scuffed and boasted. . . ."

From Mirador Crescent, follow this street as it loops back to Walter Road and walk back along Uplands Crescent. Turn right on a street called The Grove and follow it to a tree-lined area with the same name. Thomas loved the Grove for its quiet, woodsy atmosphere surrounded by the residential neighborhood. It is the same today. In "Return Journey," he wrote: "And I went up through the White Grove, into Cwmdonkin Park, the snow still sailing and the childish, lonely, remembered music fingering on in the suddenly gentle wind." Double back to Cwmdonkin Drive, which runs along Cwmdonkin Park, and head north on it, as Thomas did many times early in life, to no. 5, where a blue plaque marks his place of birth. This part of town is the font of his earliest recollections. In an April 1934 letter to Pamela Hansford Johnson, a former girlfriend, he wrote of the view from his window at 5 Cwmdonkin Drive on a Sunday:

> Sunday in Wales. The Sunday-walkers have slunk out of the
> warrens in which they sleep and breed all the unholy week,
> have put on their black suits, reddest eyes, and meanest expres-
> sions, and are now marching up the hill past my window.

Continue along Cwmdonkin Drive until you reach Terrace Road; turn left onto the road. The upper entrance to Cwmdonkin Park is ahead on the left. A stone memorial to Thomas was placed in the park in 1963 and is carved with the closing lines from "Fern Hill":

> Oh as I was young and easy in the mercy of his means,
> Time held me green and dying
> Though I sang in my chains like the sea.

For the young Thomas, Cwmdonkin Park was a safe yet wild outpost, a controlled yet uninhibited sanctuary. Here, he would roam the hilly grass, skirt the ponds and streams, and play make-believe with his fellow adventurers. It was the place that freed him from the puritanical, devotional environment of The Uplands, where the pubgoers were separated from the churchgoers. In "Reminiscences of Childhood," Thomas describes what the park meant to him:

[T]he park itself was a world within the world of the sea town;
quite near where I lived, so near that on summer evenings I
could listen, in my bed, to the voices of other children playing
ball on the sloping, paper-littered bank; the park was full of ter-
rors and treasures. . . . And that park grew up with me; that
small, interior world widened as I learned its names and its
boundaries; as I discovered new refuges and ambushes in its
miniature woods and jungles, hidden homes and lairs for the
multitudes of the young, for cowboys and Indians. . . .

Return to Uplands Crescent by turning left on Glanmor Road and walking
downhill. Glanmor Road becomes Uplands Crescent.

THOMAS WALK 2, *Laugharne*

Sites Featured: The Boat House, Carmarthen Bay, Thomas's writing shed, and St. Martin's Church. *Distance*: About 4 miles. *Degree of Difficulty*: Easy to moderate. *Time*: Half day. *Starting Point*: St. Martin's Church. *See Map*.

The town of Laugharne (pronounced *larn*), the river, the nature walks, and the surrounding hills are Welsh countryside at its best. It is best reached by car—although there are buses to Laugharne from Swansea and also from Carmarthen, the other city closest to Laugharne located about thirty miles northwest of Swansea, but they run very infrequently. Walk into town from St. Martin's Churchyard along King Street. Laugharne is called Llaregub in *Under Milk Wood*,

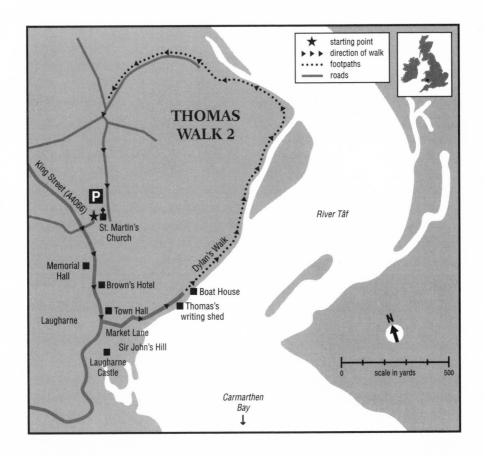

and if you have any doubts about that, the locals will soon correct you. They'll point to the fact that the theater company in town is called The Llaregub Players, and that they were the first amateur company to perform *Under Milk Wood* in Laugharne at Memorial Hall. As you walk along King Street you'll see Memorial Hall as well as Brown's Hotel—the place with the most Thomas associations in town; this is where he often had his last drink of the night before heading up the path to the Boat House where he and Caitlin lived.

Thomas loved Laugharne deeply. In a description he wrote of the town for the British Broadcasting Company in the late 1940s, he conveys the riches of this small yet timeless place. These are the first and last paragraphs:

> Off and on, up and down, high and dry, man and boy, I've been living now for fifteen years, or centuries, in this timeless, beautiful, barmy town, in this far, forgetful, important place of herons, cormorants (known here as billyduckers), castle, churchyard, gulls, ghosts, geese, feuds, scares, scandals, cherry-trees, mysteries, jackdaws in the chimneys, bats in the belfry, skeletons in the cupboards, pubs, mud, cockles, flatfish, curlews, rain, and human, often all too human, beings; and, though still very much a foreigner, I am hardly ever stoned in the streets anymore, and can claim to be able to call several of the inhabitants, and a few of the herons, by their Christian names.
>
> . . .
>
> They envy Laugharne its minding of its own, strange business; its sane disregard for haste; its generous acceptance of the follies of others, having so many, ripe and piping, of its own; its insular, featherbed air; its philosophy of "It will all be the same in a hundred years' time." They deplore its right to be, in their eyes, so wrong, and to enjoy it so much as well. And, through envy and indignation, they label and libel it a legendary lazy little black-magical bedlam by the sea. And is it? Of course not, I hope.

The highlight of this walk around Laugharne and the one with the most memorable views is a path now named Dylan's Walk, from the estuary mouth of Carmarthen Bay to the Boat House. The views of the bay are spectacular, and the sea air crisp and clean, with birds constantly whirling overhead. Continue walking south along King Street to Laugharne's Town Hall. Turn left at the hall onto Market Lane; farther along, Market Lane will become Dylan's Walk and lead you right to Thomas's writing shed.

The shed is painted bright blue, and the view from the shed stretches across the estuary to the hills across the way and out to Carmarthen Bay. The shed is almost surrounded by the bay. Inside, it is arranged to look as it did when Thomas wrote there: a chaotic mess, with books, papers, dirt, and an old rick-

Figure 13. Inside Dylan Thomas's writing shed. Laugharne, Dyfed, Wales.

Figure 14. The Thomas Boat House. Laugharne, Dyfed, Wales.

ety table and chairs littering the one room. The quarters are sparse but were sufficient for Thomas, who was drawn there by the peace and the calming effect of the water. Caitlin describes him working in the shed in her book written after his death: "Then, blown up with muck and somnolence, up to his humble shed, nesting high above the estuary; and bang into intensive scribbling, muttering, whispering, intoning, bellowing and juggling of words; till seven o'clock prompt."

A few hundred yards up the path is the Boat House. The entrance to the house is through the garden, and every deck and every window has a magnificent view of the estuary, which Thomas always described as "heron-priested." His poem "Over Sir John's Hill," from which the following two stanzas are excerpted, evokes this view:

> Heron, mirrored, go,
> As the snapt feathers snow,
> Fishing in the tear of the Towy. Only a hoot owl
> Hollows, a glassblade blow in cupped hands, in the looted elms,
>
> And no green cocks or hens
> Shout
> Now on Sir John's hill. The heron, ankling the scaly
> Lowlands of the waves,
> Makes all the music; and I who hear the tune of the slow,
> Wear-willow river, grave,
> Before the lunge of the night, the notes this time-shaken
> Stone for the sake of the souls of the slain birds sailing.

Sir John's Hill is the small hill behind Thomas's shed, and the Towy is a river that flows into the estuary.

From the Boat House continue walking up the path until it turns inland and returns to town. Head back to St. Martin's Church, where Thomas and Caitlin are buried in a grave marked by a simple wooden cross with only their names and dates recorded on it. Within the church is a replica of the plaque at the Poets' Corner in Westminster Abbey dedicated to Thomas. It contains these lines, which appear in *Quite Early One Morning*: "And some like myself, just came, one day, for the day, and never left; got off the bus, and forget to get on again."

PRIMARY READINGS

Thomas, Dylan. *Adventures in the Skin Trade*. New York: W. W. Norton, 1969.

———. *A Child's Christmas in Wales*. New York: New Directions, 1997.

————. *The Collected Stories*. New York: W. W. Norton, 1986.

————. *Dylan Thomas: The Loud Hill of Wales, Poetry of Place*. Selected by Walford Davies. London: J. M. Dent and Sons, 1991.

————. *A Dylan Thomas Treasury: Poems, Stories, and Broadcasts*. Selected by Walford Davies. London: J. M. Dent and Sons, 1991.

————. *The Poems of Dylan Thomas*. New York: W. W. Norton, 1979.

————. *Portrait of the Artist as a Young Dog*. New York: W. W. Norton, 1975.

————. *Quite Early One Morning*. New York: New Directions, 1960.

————. *Under Milk Wood, A Play for Voices*. New York: W. W. Norton, 1984.

8

James Joyce's Dublin

*I want to give a picture of Dublin so complete that if the
city one day suddenly disappeared from the earth it could
be reconstructed out of my book.*

—JAMES JOYCE to Frank Budgen,
James Joyce and the Making of Ulysses

James Joyce (1882–1941) loved—and at the same time hated—Dublin, the city
of his birth. And for many years Dublin returned the ambivalent passions of
its most famous son. Dublin's feelings toward Joyce, however, have changed
in the last ten years or so. Now, in the center of town, just off O'Connell Street,
is a life-size statue of Joyce, and his bust adorns St. Stephen's Green, a city
park featured in his works. Excerpts from his most notorious novel, *Ulysses*,
appear on plaques in the concrete of sidewalks and walking lanes. And,
unthinkable in another era, in the middle of O'Connell Street—the quintessential Dublin thoroughfare—there stands a statue of Anna Livia, the goddess
of the River Liffey and an obvious representation of *Finnegans Wake*'s Anna
Livia Plurabelle.

For years Joyce was neglected by his native city. He was, in fact, reviled; after
all, he wrote that "dirty book," *Ulysses* (1922), which was banned in both Britain
and the United States for explicit sexual passages. In a historic 1933 decision Judge
John M. Woolsey lifted the ban in the United States; this decision soon also led
to the book's free circulation in Britain. Today, *Ulysses* is recognized as a masterpiece and was, in fact, recently selected by a panel of scholars and writers as
the finest English-language novel published in the twentieth century. Ironies mul-
tiply endlessly in the case of Joyce and Dublin, and the writer known for his use
of irony and humor in literature would have enjoyed every minute of it. For
instance, one of the biggest cultural celebrations in Dublin is Bloomsday, 16 June.
It marks the anniversary of the day in 1904 chronicled in *Ulysses*. Each year on
that date Dubliners dressed as characters from Joyce's novels walk the streets.

Figure 15. James Joyce Statue on Earl Street. Dublin, Ireland.

Some even dress up as Joyce himself complete with suit, hat, white shoes, and his trademark walking stick, the ashplant.

Joyce was born in Rathmines, a fashionable suburb of Dublin, on 2 February 1882. He was the first of ten children who survived at birth. His father, John Joyce, was a charismatic, talented storyteller and a singer and reprobate who "filled his house with children and with debts," as Joyce's biographer Richard Ellmann puts it. The family was forced to move repeatedly to avoid collection agencies, and each move took them deeper and deeper into poverty, eventually forcing them out of fashionable suburbs to city squalor. At age nine Joyce had to leave the prestigious Clongowes Wood College because his father could no longer pay the boarding school's tuition.

After graduating from Dublin's University College, Joyce left Dublin for Paris and, with the exception of a few brief visits home, he lived the rest of his life on the Continent. He was first recalled home in 1903 by his mother's death from cancer at age forty-four. Joyce's father sent him a telegram in Paris stating simply, "Mother dying. Come home." Joyce blamed his father for his mother's untimely death, but despite his resentments, he later recognized that he owed much of his facility with language to him.

During this first visit home, Joyce met Nora Barnacle, a country girl from Galway who worked as maid at Finn's Hotel in Dublin. His relationship with her shocked everyone. What was this intellectual doing with an uneducated maid? "She'll stick to you like a barnacle," said Joyce's father. Joyce and Nora nevertheless left Ireland together later that year. After twenty-seven years and two children, they married in London in 1931 and remained together until Joyce's death on 13 January 1941 in Zurich, Switzerland. Perhaps they had little in common intellectually, but as Joyce's letters to Nora suggest and as is often said of seemingly disparate couples, they were probably extremely compatible in the bedroom.

Though Joyce had many women friends—and received, in fact, much of his financial support from women—there is no evidence that he had any liaisons with anyone else while he was with Nora. Notoriously jealous, Joyce, on the other hand, suspected Nora of several affairs she had supposedly had before and soon after she first met him (none of which has ever been confirmed). During their thirty-seven-year relationship, they lived in several European cities, including Pola, Trieste (both then part of Austria-Hungary), Zurich, and Rome, but mostly Paris. While Joyce knew the languages of the countries where they lived and was always the center of a literary circle, Nora was left at home alone, often distraught, a stranger in a strange land. Their always strained finances only made matters worse. She once revealed in an interview that she felt that the worse thing a woman could do was to marry a writer, especially a great one. She never read any of his books; it's not even clear whether she ever read the book of poems he dedicated to her. She felt that as she was married to him, she didn't need to read what he wrote to know him.

Like many expatriates, Joyce's subject matter is home. From abroad, he wrote about Dublin in great and accurate detail. His three great novels and a book of stories all feature Dublin: *Dubliners* (stories, 1914), *A Portrait of the Artist as a Young Man* (1916), *Ulysses* (1922), and *Finnegans Wake* (1939). Joyce would often write to his brother, Stanislaus, who lived in Dublin, to ask him to check on details about particular places he wanted to feature in his books. For instance, in one letter he asked Stanislaus to go to 7 Eccles Street, Leopold Bloom's residence in *Ulysses,* and count the number of steps leading to the basement door. Despite his preoccupation with re-creating Dublin in absolute detail, Joyce's themes are universal. He writes about Dublin and, at the same time, about the whole of human experience.

In 1909 Joyce returned briefly to Dublin to try to get some money. While there, he wrote to Nora in Trieste: "How sick, sick, sick I am of Dublin! It is a city of failure, of rancour and of unhappiness. I long to be out of it." Although he rejected his native city, Joyce made it the subject of his life's work. And, from the objective distance of exile, he recognized its utter uniqueness. As he told his friend Frank Budgen during a walk in Zurich in 1918, "[W]hat a city Dublin is! I wonder if there is another like it."

JOYCE WALK 1, *South of Dublin along the coast*

Sites Featured: The house where Joyce lived as a child in Bray, Clifton School, the James Joyce Museum, Forty-Foot Gentlemen's Bathing Place, Sydney Parade, and Sandymount Strand. *Distance:* 5–6 miles. *Degree of Difficulty:* Easy to moderate. *Time:* Allow a full day. *Starting Point:* The town of Bray. *The Dublin Colour Map,* which is available at the Tourist Information Office on O'Connell Street, is an excellent map of this area. Other maps are available directly across from the Information Office at the office of Dublin Transport.

Bray can be reached from Dublin through the Dublin Area Rapid Transport (DART). Take the train from Connolly Station and exit at the town of Bray. As you exit, turn toward the sea and cross the tracks to the Esplanade. Turn left on the Esplanade and walk to Martello Terrace, a row of connected houses facing the sea. Joyce moved here with his family in 1887 at age five, already his third home. They lived at no. 1, a two-story, small wooden house—the one closest to the sea—until 1891.

This house was the setting for a heated religious debate that takes place during a Christmas dinner in *A Portrait of the Artist as a Young Man.* Highly autobiographical, the novel traces the development of the protagonist, Stephen Dedalus, from birth to age twenty, showing his evolution into the artist of the title. Joyce names his alter-ego Stephen for a Christian martyr, and Dedalus, for a character from Greek myth who escapes a labyrinth by fashioning wings for himself and flying away.

It is a troubled time in Ireland. Charles Stewart Parnell, a leader of the Irish Parliamentary Party and a staunch supporter of Irish home rule, has died. Many of his supporters, including Stephen's father, Simon Dedalus, blame his death on the attacks on him led by the Roman Catholic clergy over his affair with the then-married Mrs. Kitty O'Shea.

Stephen returns home from Clongowes Wood College, the same school Joyce attended as a boy, to spend the Christmas holiday with his parents. Considered old enough to join the elders at Christmas dinner while the other children dine in the nursery, Stephen witnesses an ugly debate between his father and his aunt Dante over Parnell:

> —O, he'll remember all this when he grows up, said Dante hotly—the language he heard against God and religion and priests in his own home.
> —Let him remember too, cried Mr Casey to her from across

> the table, the language with which the priests and the priests'
> pawns broke Parnell's heart and hounded him into his grave.
> Let him remember that too when he grows up.
>
> —Sons of bitches! cried Mr Dedalus. When he was down
> they turned on him to betray him and rend him like rats in a
> sewer. Lowlived dogs! And they look it! By Christ, they look it!

Joyce resumes Stephen's story in *Ulysses*, where Stephen is one of the main characters. The novel is the account of one day in the life of Leopold Bloom, a Jewish Dubliner married to an opera singer, Molly. While Bloom wanders the city, Molly is at home in bed waiting for her lover, Blazes Boylan, to arrive. Stephen is also about in the city and eventually he and Bloom meet. Joyce structured *Ulysses* around Homer's *The Odyssey* (about 750 B.C.), the epic story of Odysseus's (Ulysses in Latin) wanderings after the Trojan War, while his wife, Penelope, waits for him at home. Each episode in *Ulysses* corresponds in some way to an episode from *The Odyssey*.

Return to the DART station from Martello Terrace and take the train north to Dalkey, a small seaside town. In *Ulysses,* as a young man of twenty-two, Stephen teaches at a boy's school in this town called the Clifton School. The school actually existed and Joyce did, in fact, teach there himself when he, like Stephen, was twenty-two. To see the building that was once the school, turn right from the DART station onto Cunningham Road and follow it to Dalkey Avenue. Turn right on Dalkey and continue walking until you reach Old Quarry Road. On the corner of Dalkey and Old Quarry is a large, white private home called Summerfield set back under a grove of trees; this used to be the Clifton School. In the second chapter of *Ulysses* ("Nestor"), we meet the anti-Semitic headmaster Mr. Deasy at the Clifton School, who has a disagreement with Stephen over Jews, education, and a philosophical view of history. Stephen is appalled by Mr. Deasy's prejudice:

> —Mark my words, Mr Dedalus, he said. England is in the
> hands of the jews. In all the highest places: her finance, her
> press. And they are the signs of a nation's decay. . . . As sure as
> we are standing here the jew merchants are already at their
> work of destruction.
>
> . . .
>
> —A merchant, Stephen said, is one who buys cheap and
> sells dear, jew or gentile, is he not?
>
> —They sinned against the light, Mr Deasy said gravely. And
> you can see darkness in their eyes. . . .

From Old Quarry Road it is one mile to Stephen's home in Martello Tower, Sandycove, now the James Joyce Museum. To visit the tower, walk along Dalkey Avenue northeast toward the harbor, until it becomes Ulverton Road. Follow Ulverton Road until it veers to the left and becomes Briffni Road. Take Briffni Road to Sandycove Avenue East. Sandycove leads to the James Joyce Museum overlooking the sea. In chapter 2 of *Ulysses* ("Nestor"), Stephen walks from the tower to the Clifton School; the route we've followed here is Stephen's route to the school in reverse.

Martello Tower is one of many towers the British built along Great Britain's coastlines in the nineteenth century to defend against a possible invasion by Napoleonic forces. The invasion never came. The British took the name, Martello, by which all the towers are known, from a fortification on Cape Mortella in Corsica. In 1904, Oliver St. John Gogarty, a writer friend of Joyce's, rented the tower and invited Joyce and others to visit. One of the other guests, an Oxford student and Joyce's roommate at the tower, had a nightmare about a panther, grabbed a gun he had brought with him, and began shooting inside the tower where he and Joyce were sleeping. Joyce was quite shaken by the experience and left the next morning never to return. He lived there exactly one week.

Ulysses opens with a scene in this tower (which explains why the tower is named after Joyce). Stephen's mother has recently died. Joyce's own mother died in 1903, a year prior to the day *Ulysses* takes place. When the novel opens, Buck Mulligan is on the tower parapet looking out on the Irish Sea, and, as he shaves, Stephen asks him about their roommate, Haines:

> —Tell me, Mulligan, Stephen said quietly. . . . How long is Haines going to stay in this tower?
> —God, isn't he dreadful? he said frankly. A ponderous Saxon. . . . God, these bloody English. Bursting with money and indigestion. . . Because he comes from Oxford. . . .
> —He was raving all night about a black panther, Stephen said. Where is his guncase?
> —A woful lunatic, Mulligan said. Were you in a funk?
> —I was, Stephen said with energy and growing fear. Out here in the dark with a man I don't know raving and moaning to himself about shooting a black panther. . . . If he stays on here I am off.

The James Joyce Museum in the tower includes a number of Joyce's personal possessions, such as his ashplant walking stick, a vest, photos, manuscripts, letters, posters, cards, and books. You can enjoy the same view of Dublin Bay that Mulligan and Stephen looked out on, on the parapet, which is open to visitors.

The famous Forty-Foot Gentlemen's Bathing Place is at the bottom of the hill on your right. This area of Dublin Bay has traditionally been used by men as a place to bath and swim. Its called the Forty-Foot Bathing Place because the men, who usually bathe or swim naked, remove their clothing on rocks forty feet above the bay. In *Ulysses*, Stephen and Haines accompany Mulligan to the Bathing Place for his morning swim, but Stephen doesn't join him. "He capered before them down towards the fortyfoot hole, fluttering his winglike hands, leaping nimbly, Mercury's hat quivering in the fresh wind that bore back to them his brief birdlike cries."

From the tower walk up Sandycove Avenue west to the Sandycove DART Station to catch the train north toward Dublin. Take the train north six stops to Sydney Parade and get off there. This station is featured in *Dubliners*, a book of fifteen short stories all set in Dublin at the beginning of the twentieth century. Each story focuses on a different Dubliner, some of whom learn from their experiences and others who don't. One of the most poignant stories in the collection, "A Painful Case," has its climax at Sydney Parade Station. In the story, Mrs. Sinico is attracted to a bachelor, Mr. Duffy. Accompanied by her daughter, Mrs. Sinico meets Mr. Duffy at concerts and invites him to meet her husband, a sea captain. The "affair," which is limited to conversations about music and other topics of interest to both, is very innocent until a tragic misunderstanding causes Mr. Duffy to retreat to his quarters in Chapelizod, vowing never to see her again. She is humiliated by the experience and takes to drink. Four years after their separation, Mr. Duffy reads in the paper:

Death of a Lady at Sydney Parade
A PAINFUL CASE

> To-day at the City of Dublin Hospital the Deputy Coroner (in the absence of Mr Leverett) held an inquest on the body of Mrs. Emily Sinico, aged forty-three years, who was killed at Sydney Parade Station yesterday evening. The evidence showed that the deceased lady, while attempting to cross the line, was knocked down by the engine of the ten o'clock slow train from Kingstown, thereby sustaining injuries of the head and right side which led to her death.

Whether the death is an accident or a suicide is left unresolved.

From Sydney Parade Station follow Sydney Parade Road toward the coast of the Irish Sea. Turn left along the Strand and follow the coast north past another Martello Tower to Sandymount Beach. Where Sandymount becomes Beach Road, there is a freestanding monument dedicated to Joyce erected in 1983. One can see the Dublin Power Station, known as "The Pigeon Works," jutting out into the bay, a Dublin landmark.

In chapter 3 ("Proteus") of *Ulysses*, Stephen leaves Mr. Deasy, the headmaster at Clifton School, and takes a train from Dalkey to the Lansdowne Road Station. From here, he walks along Leahy Terrace to Beach Road and from there, on to Sandymount Strand. Stephen asks himself as he walks along here, "Am I walking into eternity along Sandymount Strand?" He continues his stroll along the shore:

The grainy sand had gone from under his feet. His boots trod again a damp crackling mast, razorshells, squeaking pebbles, that on the unnumberd pebbles beats, wood sieved by the ship-worm, lost Armada. Unwholesome sandflats waited to suck his treading soles, breathing upward sewage breath. He coasted them, walking warily.

Later that same day, Bloom walks along Sandymount Strand, and we read about his experiences here much later in *Ulysses* in chapter 13 ("Nausicaa"). He is sitting on the seawall watching some women and children playing in the sand. It is twilight. One of the women, Gerty MacDowell, catches his eye, and they start a flirtation conducted at a distance. Their visual flirtation is accompanied by music and chanting from a men's temperance retreat being held at the near-by Star of the Sea Church in Sandymount, which still exists and is open to visitors. The episode comes to a climax in a thunderous display of Roman candles that showers the sky.

Across from the Sandymount shore, on the corner of Strand Road and Lea Road, is a solid-looking gray stone house (no. 35) facing the sea. Joyce lived here very briefly in 1904. It remains a private residence. To visit the Star of the Sea Church, walk inland along Beach Road to Leahy's Terrace; the Sea Church is on the corner of Leahy's Terrace and Sandymount Road. The church was built in the middle of the nineteenth century and remains an active neighborhood parish today. The last time I was there, I saw a notice posted in the vestibule inviting men to a "night of song and drink-free entertainment." Perhaps these events have replaced the temperance meetings of Joyce's day. As you leave the church, walk north on Sandymount Road for about 100 yards to Tritonville Road. Turn left here, and continue along Tritonville until you reach Herbert Road. On Herbert Road turn right. Go past the Mount Herbert Hotel and continue on to the Lansdowne DART Station, across from the famous Lansdowne Rugby Ground. Board the train going north to Dublin's Connolly Station.

JOYCE WALK 2, *Dublin south of the River Liffey*

Sites Featured: St. Stephen's Green, University College, Merrion Square, Leinster House, the National Library, the National Gallery, the National Museum, Brown Thomas Department Store, Davy Byrnes's pub, Bewley's Cafe, and Trinity College. *Distance:* 4 miles. *Degree of Difficulty:* Easy to moderate. *Time:* Allow a full day. *Starting Point:* The bust of Joyce in the south side of St. Stephen's Green. See *The Dublin Colour Map*, which is available at the Tourist Information Office on O'Connell Street.

St. Stephen's Green is a park in the heart of Dublin south of the River Liffey. Grafton, Dawson, and Kildare Streets all lead from Trinity College to St. Stephen's. A good place to begin is at the bust of Joyce in the south side of the park, across from the Newman House and University College, the college from which Joyce graduated shortly before he left Ireland for the Continent. As a student, Joyce crossed St. Stephen's daily to attend classes at University College. In *A Portrait of the Artist as a Young Man*, Stephen crosses St. Stephen's on his way to French class:

> [T]he trees in Stephen's Green were fragrant of rain and the
> rainsodden earth gave forth its mortal odour, a faint incense ris-
> ing upward through the mould from many hearts. The soul of
> the gallant venal city which his elders had told him of had shrunk
> with time to a faint mortal odour rising from the earth. . . .

St. Stephen's is lush with ponds, flowers, and trees; it also has a bandstand used in the summer as well as large, open grassy areas where Dubliners will doff shirts and sweaters at the slightest sign of sun to lie white and pale under its warm glow.

From St. Stephen's Green walk south on Earlsfort Terrace to the entrance to University College. In chapter 5 of *Portrait*, Stephen and his friend Lynch break away from a student protest group to take a stroll and discuss philosophy, theories of beauty and esthetics, poetry and art, and what the world has to offer young college graduates in 1904. They walk south from the college along Adelaide Road to Leeson Street Bridge: "They had reached the [Leeson Street] canal bridge and, turning from their course, went on by the trees. A crude grey light, mirrored in the sluggish water, and a smell of wet branches over their heads seemed to war against the course of Stephen's thoughts." Follow Stephen and Lynch's route to Leeson Street Bridge. When you reach the bridge, turn left at Wilton Terrace along the canal to Mount Street Lower near Sir Patrick Dun's Hospital. When Stephen and Lynch near the hospital, "[a] long dray laden with old iron came round the corner of Sir Patrick Dun's hospital covering the end of Stephen's speech with the harsh roar of jangled and rattling metal."

Turn left on Mount Street Lower and walk, as do Stephen and Lynch, to Merrion Square. After a brief encounter with a fellow student, "[t]hey turned their faces towards Merrion Square and went on for a little in silence." Merrion Square is a well-preserved example of Georgian architecture. The Square was designed in 1762, and though on the surface the terraced houses seem alike, there is enough individuality to distinguish them from one another. Many of the doorways were photographed for the well-known poster of colorful Dublin townhouse doorways. Former occupants of the terraced houses include Oscar Wilde, who lived with his parents at no. 1, William Butler Yeats at no. 82, and George William Russell (known as A. E.) at no. 84. All are marked with plaques. A familiar Dublin story is that Yeats went to visit Russell and Russell, to visit Yeats, both leaving their houses at the same time. Yeats had his head in the clouds, Russell's eyes were on the ground, and they passed on the street without seeing each other.

Within a block or two of Merrion Square is Leinster House, which was designed as a palace for a duke in 1745–48 and later bought by the Royal Dublin Society, a pro-British group, in 1817. The Irish Parliament has occupied it since 1925. The National Library (built 1884–90), the National Gallery (built 1859–64) and the National Museum (built 1884–90) are all nearby. Stephen and Lynch's walk in *Portrait* takes them across Leinster House's lawn:

> A fine rain began to fall from the high veiled sky and they turned into the duke's [Leinster] lawn, to reach the national library before the shower came. . . .
>
> The rain fell faster. When they passed through the passage beside the royal Irish academy they found many students sheltering under the arcade of the library.

Stephen returns to the National Library another day:

> A sudden swift hiss fell from the windows above him and he [Stephen] knew that the electric lamps had been switched on in the reader's room. He turned into the pillared hall, now calmly lit, went up the staircase and passed in through the clicking turnstile.

The National Library also appears in *Ulysses* in chapter 9 ("Scylla and Charybdis"). Stephen is in the director's office engaged in an intellectual discussion about Hamlet with several scholars. Meanwhile, at the very end of chapter 8 ("Lestrygonians"), Bloom is wandering about town, in the neighborhood of the library and musuem. He is heading toward the library when he catches sight of Blazes Boylan, his wife's lover, and takes refuge in the museum:

> Mr Bloom came to Kildare Street. First I must. Library.

Straw hat in sunlight [this is Boylan]. Tan shoes. Turnedup
trousers. It is. It is.
His heart quopped softly. To the right. Museum. Goddesses.
He swerved to the right. . . .
Making for the museum gate with long windy strides he lift-
ed his eyes. Handsome building.

Bloom does later go to the library, where he crosses paths with Stephen, accompanied by Mulligan, on his way out.

From the library walk west on Molesworth Street to Grafton Street. As in
Joyce's day, Grafton Street—a pedestrian-only street—is the fashionable center
of town. It is lined with smart shops, restaurants such as Bewley's, buskers (street
musicians), and its centerpiece, the Brown Thomas Department Store. A favorite
in Joyce's day, it is a Dublin landmark. Note the plaque in the sidewalk under
the display window, which quotes from *Ulysses*. As he passes Brown Thomas in
his wanderings, Bloom considers buying Molly a pincushion for her birthday:

Grafton Street gay with housed awnings lured his senses.
Muslin prints, silk, dames and dowagers, jingle of harnesses,
hoofthuds lowringing in the baking causeway. . . .
He passed, dallying, the windows of Brown Thomas, silk
mercers. Cascades of ribbons. Flimsy China silks. A tilted urn
poured from its mouth a flood of bloodhued poplin: lustrous
blood. . . .
Pincushions. I'm a long time threatening to buy one. . . .

An excellent place to stop for refreshments in this area is Davy Byrnes's pub
(spelled "Byrne's" by Joyce) at 21 Duke Street, the alleylike street just south of
Brown Thomas. This is Joyce's "moral pub," where I was conned out of a pint
of Guinness an old Irish codger. Davy Byrnes opened the pub in 1873 and his
picture hangs over the bar to this day. Near the painting of Byrnes is one of Joyce
painted by the Irish artist Harry Kernoff. *Ulysses'* chapter 8 ("Lestrygonians") corresponds to the episode in *The Odyssey* when Odysseus and his crew encounter
the cannibalistic Lestrygonians. Feeling hungry, Bloom enters the pub:

He entered Davy Byrne's. Moral pub. . . .
—Let me see. I'll take a glass of burgundy [said Bloom]
and . . . let me see. . . . Have you a cheese sandwich?
—Yes, sir.
Like a few olives too if they have them. Italian I prefer. Good
glass of burgundy; take away that. Lubricate. A nice salad, cool
as a cucumber. Tom Kernan can dress. Puts gusto into it. Pure
olive oil. Milly served me that cutlet with a sprig of parsley.
Take one Spanish onion. God made food, the devil the cooks.
Devilled crab.

Figure 16. Davy Byrnes's pub. Dublin, Ireland.

—Wife well?

—Quite well, thanks . . . A cheese sandwich, then. Gorgonzola, have you?

—Yes, sir.

If a Gorgonzola sandwich is not to your taste, stop at Bewley's Cafe at 78–79 Grafton Street. It is a large, noisy restaurant and bakery that seems to go on room after room, each room livelier than the last. Upstairs is a James Joyce banquet room and on the top floor, near the rest rooms, is a little museum. There is another Bewley's on Great George's Street on the other side of the River Liffey, which is mentioned in the *Dubliners* story, "A Little Cloud."

After refreshments continue along Grafton Street to Nassau Street and the last stop on this walk, Trinity College, founded by Queen Elizabeth in 1592 and noted for its possession of the *Book of Kells,* a late eighth- to early ninth-century illuminated manuscript of the Gospels. Visitors can view the manuscript for a fee.

JOYCE WALK 3, *Dublin*

Sites Featured: The statue of Anna Livia, Gresham Hotel, Ambassador Cinema, Dublin Writers Museum, the James Joyce Centre, Belvedere College, St. George's Church, St. Francis Xavier Church, Joyce home on North Circular Road, and Glasneven Cemetery. *Distance:* About 3 miles. *Degree of Difficulty:* Easy to moderate. *Time:* Allow a full day. *Starting Point:* The statue of Anna Livia. See *The Dublin Colour Map*, which is available at the Tourist Information Office on O'Connell Street.

The bronze statue of Anna Livia in a stone-block fountain on O'Connell Street was erected in 1988. It is dedicated to the River Liffey, which was once known as Anna Livia, according the ancient Irish custom of giving rivers women's names. Anyone who has attempted to read *Finnegans Wake* will recognize that the statue is a representation of Anna Livia Plurabelle, a character from that work. Joyce imagines her as the goddess of the River Liffey, which flows from its source in the Wicklow Mountains through Phoenix Park and the city of Dublin and ultimately out to sea at Dublin Harbour. The statue depicts Anna Livia bathing in water, with her hair flowing down over her body, representing the cycle of birth, life, death, and rebirth. The following passage from *Finnegans Wake*, a conversation between two washerwomen, reveals her nature:

> O tell me about Anna Livia! I want to hear all about Anna Livia. Well you know Anna Livia? Yes, of course, we all know Anna Livia. Tell me all. Tell me now. You'll die when you hear. . . .
>
> And there she was, Anna Livia, she darent catch a winkle of sleep, purling around like the chit of a child, Wendawanda, a finger-thick, in a Lapsummer skirt and damazon cheeks, for to ishim bonzour to her dear dubber Dan. . . .
>
> First she let her hair fall down and it flussed to her feet its teviots winding coils. Then, mother-naked, she sampood herself with galawater and fraguant pistania mud, wupper and lauar, from crown to sole. . . .

Walk north along O'Connell Street and cross the street to the porticoed General Post Office Building, which was occupied by Irish volunteers during the 1916 Easter Rebellion. The building was shelled and gutted by a British gunboat and later restored to its present condition. Inside is a marvelous statue of the mythological Celtic hero Cuchulain.

Cross over O'Connell again and walk to the Gresham Hotel at 23 Upper O'Connell Street. In the last story of *Dubliners*, "The Dead," Gabriel and Gretta Conroy, a married couple, spend the night at the Gresham Hotel after an annual Christmas dinner party and dance. It is the site of one of the most beautiful and poignant epiphanies in all of Joyce's work. In their room at the hotel, Gretta tells Gabriel about a boy who loved her when she lived with her grandmother in Galway before coming to Dublin and meeting Gabriel. The boy, Michael Furey, suffered from poor health, and the night before Gretta left for a Dublin convent school, he came to her house in the rain. He told her he didn't want to live. A week after she arrived in the convent school, Gretta heard that he had died. She tells Gabriel, " 'I think he died for me.' " Gabriel realizes how small a part he has played in his wife's life, much smaller, at least, than he ever imagined, and the somewhat pompous intellectual is humbled by this new insight. After his wife cries herself to sleep in their room at the hotel, Gabriel reflects on the meaning of what he has learned:

> Generous tears filled Gabriel's eyes. He had never felt like
> that himself towards any woman, but he knew that such a feel-
> ing must be love. . . . His soul had approached that region
> where dwell the vast hosts of the dead. He was conscious of,
> but could not apprehend, their wayward and flickering exis-
> tence. His own identity was fading out into a grey impalpable
> world: the solid world itself which these dead had one time
> reared and lived in was dissolving and dwindling.

Continue walking up O'Connell Street to Parnell Street. Note the Ambassador Cinema on the northwest corner. This was called the Rotunda Concert Rooms in Joyce's time and was where, in the *Dubliners* story "A Painful Case," Mr. Duffy met Mrs. Sinico (see Joyce Walk 1). Proceed along Parnell Square east to the Dublin Writers Museum at 18/19 Parnell Square North. This museum has various exhibits on famous Irish writers, including Joyce, Oscar Wilde, William Butler Yeats, and Samuel Beckett. Walk back down to Parnell Street and turn left on North Great George's Street. Locate no. 35, the James Joyce Centre, an eighteenth-century Georgian home that has been converted into a museum by Joyce's nephew. On display here is the door from the now-destroyed 7 Eccles Street, Bloom's fictional home.

On the corner of Denmark and North Great George's Street is Belvedere College, where Joyce attended middle school. Joyce distinguished himself here as a first-rate student and earned Ireland's equivalent of a high school diploma. Many of what we might assume to be his own experiences here are recounted in *Portrait*. For example, Stephen, as a student, attends a religious retreat at Belvedere College, where the priest terrorizes the boys with visions of the damned:

> "O, how terrible is the lot of those wretched beings! The blood
> seethes and boils in the veins, the brains are boiling in the skull,
> the heart in the breast glowing and bursting, the bowels a redhot
> mass of burning pulp, the tender eyes flaming like molten balls.

Stephen, who had begun visiting prostitutes before attending the retreat, believes the entire lecture is directed toward him. It has a devasting impact on him and, later that evening, he goes to a church and confesses his sins.

Continue northeast on Denmark Street and turn left on Temple, which will take you to Hardwicke Place. The actual 7 Eccles Street residence, Bloom and Molly's home in *Ulysses,* was located on the next block but has unfortunately long since been destroyed. The New Mater Private Hospital was erected in its place; the site, however, is commemorated with a plaque. Joyce apparently once knew the family that lived there, but not particularly well. The house's proximity to the Protestant St. George's Church, now a theater, may have been one of the reasons Joyce chose it as the setting of Bloom's home, as the church features so prominently in *Ulysses.* For instance, the Blooms hear the church's pealing of the bells every fifteen minutes. Chapter 4, "Calypso," ends with Leopold's listening to the bells: "A creak and a dark whirr in the air high up. The bells of George's church. They tolled the hour: loud dark iron."

The bells appear again at the very end of the book in the famous Molly Bloom monologue, where she keeps time by the sound of the bells: "Wait theres Georges church bells wait 3 quarters the hour 1 wait 2 o'clock well thats a nice hour of the night for him [Bloom] to be coming home at to anybody climbing down into the area if anybody saw him Ill knock him off that little habit tomorrow."

Mater Misericordiae Hospital, now part of the New Mater Private Hospital, remains on Eccles Street, as does O'Rourke's pub, now called the James Joyce Lounge. Bloom passes this pub on his way along Dorset Street, where he stops to buy a kidney at Dlugacz's for his breakfast.

Continue northeast on Dorset Street for one block to Gardiner Street and turn right. Here, you'll find St. Francis Xavier Church. This church is mentioned in the *Dubliners* story "Grace," where it is the site for a "business men's retreat": "The transept of the Jesuit Church in Gardiner Street was almost full; and still at every moment gentlemen entered from the side-door and, directed by the lay-brother, walked on tiptoe along the aisles until they found seating accommodation." The church also appears in *Ulysses,* chapter 10 ("The Wandering Rocks"). Father Conmee, S. J., a priest at St. Francis, leaves the rectory everyday and heads for Mountjoy Square: "The superior, the very reverend John Conmee S. J., reset his smooth watch in his interior pocket as he came down the presbytery steps. Five to three. Just nice time to walk to Artane."

Walk along Gardiner Street to Mountjoy Square and turn left on Fitzgibbon Street, the very first corner in the square. Fitzgibbon leads to North Circular Road; make a right here. From North Circular Road it is two short blocks to Richmond Street, a dead-end street. Cross to the other side of Richmond and make a left. Joyce lived with his family at 17 North Richmond Street, now part of North Circular Road, from 1894 to 1898, while he was attending Belvedere College. Joyce describes the street in one of the most widely read stories in *Dubliners,* "Araby," a story about a young boy whose affections for a neighborhood girl are misused by her:

> North Richmond Street, being blind, was a quiet street
> except at the hour when the Christian Brothers' School set the
> boys free. An uninhabited house of two storeys stood at the
> blind end, detached from its neighbors in a square ground. The
> other houses of the street, conscious of decent lives within
> them, gazed at one another with brown imperturbable faces.

The Christian Brothers' School still exists on North Richmond Street. Later in the story the narrator continues:

> The cold air stung us and we played till our bodies glowed. Our
> shouts echoed in the silent street. The career of our play
> brought us through the dark muddy lanes behind the houses
> where we ran the gauntlet of the rough tribes from the cottages,
> to the back doors of the dark dripping gardens where odours
> arose from the ashpits, to the dark odorous stables where a
> coachman smoothed and combed the horse or shook music
> from the buckled harness.

From here the walk is more than a mile, so you may want to take the Prospect bus on the corner of North Circular Road and Dorset Street to Prospect Park, where the next stop on this walk, Glasneven Cemetery, is located. Joyce's parents are buried here; he and his own family are buried in Zurich. Although the Irish once tried to have his remains brought to Ireland, Nora insisted that Joyce would have preferred to remain in Zurich. Other famous Irish writers are interred in this cemetary as well.

Joyce made Glasneven Cemetery famous in *Ulysses*. In chapter 6 ("Hades"), Bloom is a part of the funeral cortege for Paddy Dignam, a friend and fellow Dubliner. The cortege follows a clearly defined path through Dublin from Irishtown, to Ringsend, past Trinity College, up O'Connell Street, to Phibsborough Road, and onto Finglas Road. The other men in the carriage suddenly grow silent when they see a hearse heading away from the cemetery: "In silence they drove along Phibsborough road. An empty hearse trotted by, coming from the cemetery: looks relieved."

To return to Dublin, take the bus that travels into the city center in front of the cemetery on Fingal's Road. It will take you back to O'Connell Street.

PRIMARY READINGS

Joyce, James. *Dubliners*. New York: Bantam Classics, 1990.

———. *Finnegans Wake*. New York: Penguin, 1982.

————. *A Portrait of the Artist as a Young Man.* New York: Bantam Classics, 1992.

————. *Selected Joyce Letters.* Edited by Richard Ellmann. Oxford: Oxford University Press, 1982.

————. *Ulysses.* New York: Random House, 1986.

9

Yeats's Western Ireland

She [Yeats's mother] would spend hours listening to stories
or telling stories of the pilots and fishing people of Rosses
Point, or of her own Sligo girlhood, and it was always
assumed between her and us that Sligo was more beautiful
than other places. I can see now that she had great depths
of feeling. . . .

—W. B. Yeats, *Reveries over Childhood and Youth*

Widely considered the greatest English language poet of the twentieth century, William Butler Yeats (1865–1939) produced a body of work that has earned him the praise of both critics and ordinary readers. Although he pursued esoteric studies all his life—theosophy, folklore, spiritualism, Neoplatonism—his most powerful poems communicate the power of his vision even to those readers who know nothing of his complex symbolism.

Three cities were important to Yeats and each are present in his poetry: London, Dublin, and Sligo. Born near Dublin in Sandymount on 13 June, he spent his childhood and early manhood traveling among these cities. County Sligo, located in the west of Ireland and the site for the three walks described here, was the birthplace of his mother, Elizabeth Pollexfen. A wealthy merchant family, the Pollexfens were a practical people from the Sligo countryside; they were originally from Devon but had been in Sligo for several generations. Yeats spent much of his childhood here with his mother's family in the country and the nearby seaport, and his later interest in Irish legend and mythology can be traced back to the time he spent here.

Travelers to the west of Ireland are often stunned by the number of undisturbed megalithic monuments. This prehistoric landscape spawned the great myths and legends of ancient Ireland, which Yeats came to know intimately. Throughout his life Yeats returned to Sligo, physically and spiritually. He once wrote, "[t]o leave here is to leave beauty behind."

Unlike Yeats's mother, who was rooted in the physical world of common Irish life, Yeats's father, John Butler Yeats, was a cosmopolitan intellectual. According to Richard Ellmann in *Yeats: The Man and the Masks*, "the man [Yeats's father] talked all the time and the woman [Yeats's mother] hardly at all. . . . She had few opinions about anything, but liked best of all to exchange ghost and fairy stories." Trained in law, the father gave up his career to dedicate himself to painting, and he also ran well-known literary salons. His influence on Yeats was profound. There was a constant discussion of ideas from a broad spectrum of viewpoints, and the importance of the arts was instilled in Yeats from an early age.

On completing high school, Yeats enrolled in art school and tried his hand at painting, with poetry and writing only as secondary interests. After three years, however, he abandoned painting to focus completely on his writing. It fell to Yeats's brother, Jack Butler Yeats, who became a renowned artist of Irish landscape and rural scenes, to follow in their father's footsteps.

In London in the 1890s, Yeats met the important poets of his day and was one of the founders of the Rhymers' Club. It was here, too, that he first met Madame Helena Blavatsky, a Russian-born American who introduced him to her theories of the occult. Fascinated by her ideas, Yeats, as well as many other artists (the Russian painter Wassily Kandinsky among them), joined her Esoteric Section of the Theosophical Society. Yeats would remain a lifelong student of arcane studies. Drawing on a variety of sources that included the cosmology of the English poet, painter, engraver, and mystic William Blake, and in some instances reaching as far back as pre-Platonic ideology, he elaborated in his middle years a complex system of symbols that he used to shape his poetic imagery.

During this period, in 1889, Yeats met Maud Gonne, an actress famed for her great beauty and her intense Irish nationalism. Yeats fell desperately in love with her, referring to the moment they met as "the most troubling of [his] life." She is almost always present in his poems celebrating female beauty or those that are addressed to a beloved woman. In his poems she is goddess and temptress, ingenue and queen. It remained a hopeless love, however, as she did not return his feelings and repeatedly refused to marry him. Her marriage to the Irish nationalist John MacBride in 1903 was a painful shock to Yeats.

By this time Yeats had also met Lady Augusta Gregory, a writer and supporter of Irish literature. Her influence on Yeats was great, and she became for him a source of financial as well as intellectual support. Yeats saw her aristocratic life—particularly her life at her country home, Coole Park—as a means of creating an idealized order out of life's chaos. It was through Lady Gregory's influence that Yeats, together with George Moore, Edward Martyn, and Lady Gregory herself, became involved in the founding of the Irish National Theatre in 1898, later reorganized as Dublin's world-famous Abbey Theatre.

Both Maud Gonne and Lady Gregory encouraged and inspired Yeats's commitment to Irish nationalism. The Irish nationalist movement, which Yeats championed throughout his life, had its deepest sources in the west and spread across the island to Dublin. This was the movement that would eventually separate the small, oppressed island from England and lead to the founding of the Irish Free State.

Yeats's active participation in the everyday business of the Irish National Theatre—the political problems of censorship, the economic ones of paying bills, and the general difficulties of managing personalities—influenced his poetry and led him to produce some of his most stirring poems. He was beginning to become an important public figure. Nevertheless, Yeats's frustrations with the popular response to the theater's productions and his defeat in several public controversies he became involved in took their toll; in 1915—disillusioned and embittered—he left Ireland for England. He was not long gone when Ireland's Easter Rebellion of 1916 erupted; the rebellion and Maud Gonne's urging persuaded him to return to his homeland.

With renewed nationalistic ardor, Yeats bought and renovated a sixteenth-century Norman tower on Lady Gregory's property south of Galway. The tower, which he renamed Thoor Ballylee and where he spent many of his summers, became a central symbol in his later poetry. The same year he bought the tower, 1917, he married Georgie Hyde-Lees. His wife, who claimed to have the gift of automatic writing, gave new impetus to his belief in the occult. Based on her writings, Yeats began to sketch out the symbolic system that he outlined in his book, *A Vision* (1925), and that he employed in his poetry in a variety of ways. This system—complex, difficult, and esoteric—involves theories about history and personalities, all related to different phases of the moon.

From 1922 to 1928, Yeats served as a senator of the newly founded Irish State; in 1923 he was awarded the Nobel Prize. He had become an acknowledged national and literary figure. These years also saw Yeats at the height of his poetic powers. In 1928 he published *The Tower* and in 1933, *The Winding Stair,* two collections that include his best, most mature work. His poems, complex and multileveled, require sensitive reading; some also require knowledge of the symbolism he explains in *A Vision,* without which some of his poems would be incoherent. Yeats's habit of revising his work in later editions adds to the challenge, but also enriches one's understanding of Yeats's development as a poet.

Yeats died in January 1939 in France. As he requested in his poem "Under Ben Bulben," his body was returned to Ireland and buried at Drumcliff Churchyard in County Sligo.

YEATS WALK 1, *South of Sligo*

Sites Featured: Knocknarea, the Alt, Carrowmore Megalithic Cemetery, the "Salley Gardens," and the "Lake Isle of Innisfree." *Driving Distance:* About 25 miles. *Walking Distance:* About 5 miles. *Degree of Difficulty:* Easy to moderate, though climbing Knocknarea in the wind and rain can be challenging. *Time:* Allow a full day. *Starting Point:* Knocknarea. *See Map.*

Knocknarea, a flat-topped mountain over 1,000 feet high, is the site of a Bronze Age passage grave. The grave sits at the mountain's top and is a small hill of stones and rocks that looks like a knob from afar. To get to it from Sligo, take R292 (the same road that leads to Sligo Airport) west toward Strandhill.

Some say this is the grave of the Celtic Queen Maeve (Shakespeare's Queen Mab), who ruled over Connacht and was responsible for the death of the Irish warrior-hero Cuchulain. It is also said that those buried in the stony monument were interred standing up. Yeats makes a reference to this legend in the first stanza of the refrain of his poem, "The Black Tower":

> There in the tomb stand the dead upright,
> But winds come up from the shore:
> They shake when the winds roar,
> Old bones upon the mountain shake.

It's a steady climb up Knocknarea, mucky in areas with a tall fence to climb over along the way, but it is well worth the effort. The cairn at the top was once eighty feet high, but between visitors taking stones from it and erosion, it has diminished in size. From the eastern side of the mountain, there is a magnificent view of Rosses Point (a point of land that juts out into Sligo Bay), Sligo, and Ben Bulben mountain across the valley.

From Knocknarea, drive a bit farther along R292 to Primrose Grange, a farm. Just before the road falls away, on the left, there are bushes and a gate—almost like a notch in the hillside. The spot is grown over completely with trees, wild flowers, and ferns. Park here and walk through the dense canopy of trees known locally as the Alt. In his poem, "Man and the Echo," Yeats describes this glen:

> In a cleft that's christened Alt
> Under broken stone I halt
> At the bottom of a pit
> That broad noon has never lit,
> And shout a secret to the stone.

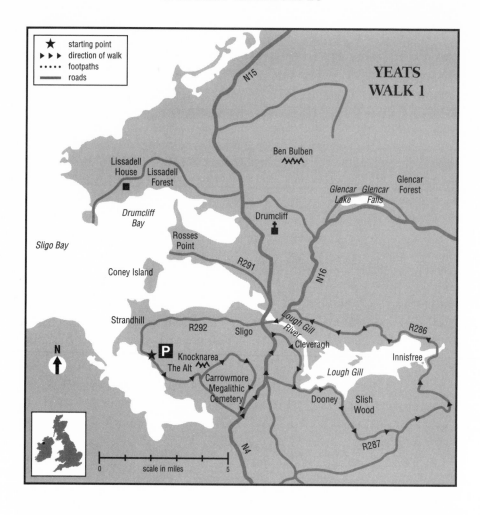

Return to R292 and continue along it until you reach a crossroads with a sign for Carrowmore Megalithic Cemetery. Take this road to the cemetery. Carrowmore is one of the largest prehistoric cemeteries in Europe. Although some of the tombs have been excavated, many remain untouched. Dolmens and tumuli dating as far back as 4,000 B.C. are everywhere. The grave mounds are believed to be those of the Firbolgs, a people thought to be the ancient colonizers of Ireland. The cemetery appears in many of Yeats's writings, including *Mythology, Fairy and Folk Tales of Ireland*, his poem "The Wind Among the Reeds," and the series of Celtic Twilight stories. In his poem "The Wanderings of Oisin," a story about an Irish poet, Oisin describes the west of Ireland before Christianity to the time of St. Patrick. In one passage he says:

> Caoilte, and Conan, and Finn were there,
> When we followed a deer with our baying hounds,

> With Bran, Sceolan, and Lomair,
> And passing the Firbolgs' burial-mounds,
> Came to the cairn-heaped grassy hill
> Where passionate Maeve is stony-still.

Leave Carrowmore Megalithic Cemetery and rejoin R292 south of Sligo. Continue on R292 until you reach the main highway to Sligo, N4. Turn left onto N4 and follow it north back toward Sligo. Look for the road signposted Cleveragh and exit here turning right onto the road. Just south of Cleveragh and along the Lough Gill River is a wild garden of ferns, reeds, and willow trees. In *Reveries over Childhood and Youth*, Yeats describes "walking from Sligo to Slishwood Forest and Lough Gill and returning to Sligo on long summer afternoons." Here grow the reedy Salley rods once used in basket making. The locals say this is the salley garden of Yeats's poem "Down by the Salley Gardens," which is also the basis for a popular Irish folk song:

> Down by the salley gardens my love and I did meet;
> She passed the salley gardens with little snow-white feet.
> She bid me take love easy, as the leaves grow on the tree;
> But I, being young and foolish, with her would not agree.
>
> In a field by the river my love and I did stand,
> And on my leaning shoulder she laid her snow-white hand.
> She bid me take life easy, as the grass grows on the weirs;
> But I was young and foolish, and now am full of tears.

From the garden continue along the road and turn east onto R287. Remain on R287 as it travels around Slish Wood and becomes R286. Near the far eastern side of Lough Gill, watch for a turnoff that leads to a small island just off the shore of the lake. This is Yeats's Lake Isle of Innisfree, whose Gaelic name is Inis Fraoich, or Heather Island. When he was a boy, Yeats's father read to him from Henry David Thoreau's *Walden Pond, or a Life in the Woods,* and the young Yeats became entranced with the idea of living alone in communion with nature. He wrote the poem "The Lake Isle of Innisfree" years later in 1890 while living in London:

> I will arise and go now, and go to Innisfree,
> And a small cabin build there, of clay and wattles made:
> Nine bean-rows will I have there, a hive for the honey-bee,
> And live alone in the bee-loud glade.
>
> And I shall have some peace there, for peace comes dropping slow,
> Dropping from the veils of the morning to where the cricket sings;
> There midnight's all a glimmer, and noon a purple glow,
> And evening full of the linnet's wings.
>
> I will arise and go now, for always night and day

I hear lake water lapping with low sounds by the shore;
While I stand on the roadway, or on the pavements grey,
I hear it in the deep heart's core.

    To return to Sligo, retrace your path back to R286 and take it west right into Sligo.

YEATS WALK 2, *Sligo*

Sites Featured: Glencar Falls, Ben Bulben, Lissadell House, Drumcliff Church and Churchyard, and Rosses Point. *Driving Distance:* About 30 miles, depending upon side trips. *Walking Distance:* 3–5 miles. *Degree of Difficulty:* Easy to moderate; the climb up Ben Bulben, however, is steep. *Time:* Allow a full day. *Starting Point:* Glencar Forest. *See Map.*

If you are coming from Sligo, take N16 heading northeast about 10 miles out of Sligo until you reach the signpost for Glencar Forest. Park in the parking area just off the road and follow the nature trail signposted Glencar Falls that begins at the parking lot. Watch your footing approaching the falls, as the path tends to be slippery underfoot.

Yeats refers to these falls in his haunting poem, "The Stolen Child." Following are the last two stanzas:

> Where the wandering water gushes
> From the hills above Glen-Car,
> In pools among the rushes
> That scarce could bathe a star,
> We seek for slumbering trout
> And whispering in their ears
> Give them unquiet dreams;
> Leaning softly out
> From ferns that drop their tears
> Over the young streams.
> *Come away, O human child!*
> *To the waters and the wild*
> *With a faery, hand in hand,*
> *For the world's more full of weeping*
>   *than you can understand.*
>
> Away with us he's going,
> The solemn-eyed:
> He'll hear no more the lowing
> Of the calves on the warm hillside
> Or the kettle on the hob
> Sing peace into his breast,
> Or see the brown mice bob
> Round and round the oatmeal-chest.
> *For he comes, the human child,*

To the waters and the wild
With a faery, hand in hand,
From a world more full of weeping
than he can understand.

This poem draws on the Irish myth of the Sidhe (pronounced *shee*), a fairy people that are believed to lure away beautiful children, especially boys. Mothers in this part of rural Ireland have dressed boys as girls probably as far back as the seventh century A.D. to try to thwart the Sidhe. Even to this day, many mothers will not praise their child to a stranger for fear that it will make their child more attractive to the Sidhe. Infants are especially protected at Halloween, as some rural people still believe that the Sidhe are out in force this night.

Walks in Glencar Forest are among the best you can take in the west of Ireland—you'll want to spend some time here exploring.

Return to N16 and drive west a few miles along the southern side of Glencar

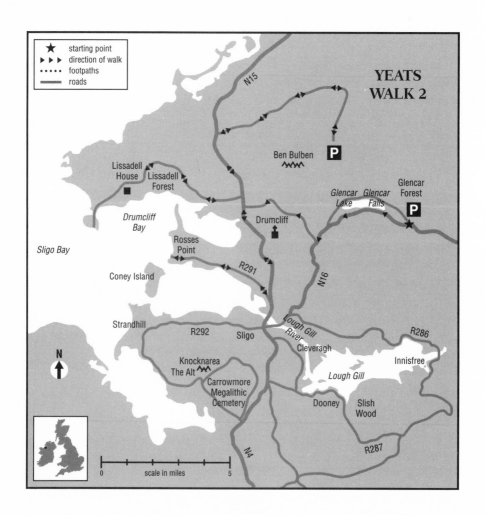

Lake as if heading back to Sligo. Past the lake and just before N16 begins to head south, turn off on a road that heads west. This road will intersect with N15. Take N15 north and exit onto a road signposted Ben Bulben—a great and, to many, a sacred mountain. The road ends at a parking area, and a beautiful nature trail continues from there to the foot of Ben Bulben. According to the Celtic story, "The Wild Boar," Ben Bulben was the hunting ground of the giant Finn Mac-Cool and his warriors, the Fianna, who hunted a wild, magical boar that wreaked havoc on the world. There is a small opening in the limestone of the mountain that Yeats imagined as the place where the pagan warriors emerge in all their fury to do battle. He describes these fierce people in his poem "Under Ben Bulben":

> Swear by those horsemen, by those women
> Complexion and form prove superhuman,
> That pale, long-visaged company
> That air in immortality
> Completeness of their passions won;
> Now they ride the wintry dawn
> Where Ben Bulben sets the scene.

In the legend Finn's betrothed, Grainnie, is in love with another man: Diarmait (many variant spellings of these names exist). Their legendary love story takes place on Ben Bulben. After Diarmait defeats many of Finn's men in battle, Finn proposes a truce and convinces Diarmait to join him in the hunt for the boar. Diarmait slays the boar, but Finn tricks him into stepping on one of the poisoned bristles in the boar's skin, thereby killing him.

The path from the nature trail up Ben Bulben is steep and dangerous because the limestone is fragile. However, if you're feeling up to the challenge, check first with the Sligo Tourist Information Office for details on the condition of the trails, availability of maps showing the safest approaches, and to see whether any guided tours are scheduled.

After visiting Ben Bulben, return to N15 and go south; you'll soon reach an exit for Lissadell. Turn off here and drive through Lissadell Forest to Lissadell House, a Georgian-style structure built in 1832. This was the home of the Gore-Booth family, a family of elevated social position with whom Yeats was friendly. He was especially fond of the two daughters, Eva and Constance, who were both socially active women he admired. Eva wrote poetry and helped to organize women workers in English textile factories; Constance aided in the 1916 uprising against British rule in which her husband, Count de Markiewicz, was an Irish leader. Yeats wrote a poem in their memory, "In Memory of Eva Gore-Booth and Con Markievicz," which opens with the following lines:

> The light of evening, Lissadell,
> Great windows open to the south,
> Two girls in silk kimonos, both
> Beautiful. . . .

Figure 17. W. B. Yeats's grave. Drumcliff, Country Sligo, Ireland.

The Gore-Booth family still owns the house, but it is open to visitors.

Return to N15 from Lissadell and take it south a short way to Drumcliff. From the road you'll see the church and graveyard where Yeats is buried. Ben Bulben looms above the landscape just beyond Drumcliff. The famous epitaph on his tombstone is the last verse of "Under Ben Bulben":

> Under bare Ben Bulben's head
> In Drumcliff churchyard Yeats is laid.
> An ancestor was rector there
> Long years ago, a church stands near,
> By the road an ancient cross.
> No marble, no conventional phrase;
> On limestone quarried near the spot
> By his command these words are cut:
> > *Cast a cold eye*
> > *On life, on death.*
> > *Horseman, pass by!*

The ancestor Yeats refers to who was a rector at Drumcliff was his great-grand-father, the Reverend William Butler Yeats (1806–1862). The ancient cross he mentions is the Celtic cross in a circle that still stands by the road leading to the church. It is practically all that remains of an early Christian monastery founded in A.D. 575.

From Drumcliff continue south on N15 in the direction of Sligo. Before entering Sligo turn right onto R291. The road is signposted Rosses Point. The end of the Rosses peninsula, which juts out into Drumcliff Bay, is two or three miles down the road. Yeats often refers to Rosses Point in his *Reveries over Childhood and Youth*; the frontispiece for that book is, in fact, a painting of Rosses Point by his brother called "Memory Harbour." When Yeats was about eight, his father took him to a grassy area on the approach to Rosses Point to read to him: "Between Sligo and Rosses Point, there is a tongue of coarse grass that runs out into the sea or the mud according to the state of the tide. It is the place where dead horses are buried. Sitting there my father read me 'The Lays of Rome.'" The buoy here still sounds the "low note" referred to in Yeats's poem, "Alternative Song for the Severed Head in 'The King of the Great Clock Tower'":

> Saddle and ride, I heard a man say,
> Out of Ben Bulben and Knocknarea,
> *What says the Clock in the great Clock Tower?*
> All those tragic characters ride
> But turn the Rosses' crawling tide,
> The meet's upon the mountain-side.
> *A slow low note and an iron bell.*

To return to Sligo from Rosses Point, take R291 to N15 and follow it south into Sligo.

YEATS WALK 3, *Sligo*

Sites Featured: In the first part of this walk, the Dominican Abbey, Yeats Memorial Building, County Library Building, Sligo County Museum, and St. John's Church; in the second half, Coole House and Park and Thoor Ballylee. *Walking Distance for the First Part:* About 2–3 miles. *Difficulty:* Easy. *Driving Distance from Sligo to Coole Park and Thoor Ballylee:* About 110 miles. *Walking Distance:* About 1 mile. *Degree of Difficulty:* Easy. *Time:* Allow half a day for each trip. *Starting Point:* Each trip begins at the Sligo Tourist Information Office on Temple Street, where maps of the city are available. A map of the second part of the walk is provided here.

Set out from the Sligo Tourist Information Office on Temple Street and walk to the ruins of the Dominican Abbey (founded in 1252, destroyed 1641) at the end of Abbey Street (take Temple to The Lungy Charles, then, from there, Grattan Street into Castle Street, right into Abbey Street). The ruins, which had a deep impact on Yeats, include the nave, the choir, and a tower. Yeats wrote a story in 1897 called "The Curse of the Fires and of the Shadows" about the destruction of the Abbey. In the story Puritan troopers destroy the Abbey and massacre the monks. Later, a magical bagpiper leads the Puritans through a wood to a cliff, where, lost in the dark, they fall to their deaths.

Retrace your steps on Abbey Street, past Castle Street and Grattan Street, and turn right onto O'Connell Street. Continue along O'Connell Street until you reach Hyde Bridge Street; turn right. You'll see the Yeats Memorial Building. This is the headquarters of the Yeats Summer School, established in 1959; here, you can obtain information on seminars, tours, lectures, and dramas associated with Yeats and other Irish poets and dramatists. From the Yeats Memorial Building continue east on Hyde Bridge Street to Stephen Street, over the Garavogue River, and on to the County Library Building and the Sligo County Museum. On view at the library and museum are some of Yeats's manuscripts and letters as well as paintings by Yeats's brother, Jack Yeats, and his father, John Butler Yeats.

Follow Stephen Street back across the Garavogue River (also called Sligo River); turn right on the corner of Quay Street. The Renaissance Town Hall (built in 1864) is on your right. The Pollexfen family had commercial buildings on Wine Street and a mill down by the quay; when Yeats was young, he disembarked here whenever he returned from England. Turn left at Adelaide Street and proceed to John Street where you'll find St. John's Church. Yeats's parents were married here in 1863. In the churchyard is the Pollexfen tomb. The church is just a few hundred yards from the Sligo Tourist Information Office.

For the second half of this walk, if you are heading out from Sligo, drive south on N4. From N4 take N17 southwest just below Collooney. Follow N17 toward Galway and take the Galway bypass, N64, which later becomes N18. Continue on N18 toward Gort. South of Ardrahan Village, just before you reach Gort, turn right on the road signposted Coole Park.

Coole House, where Yeats was a frequent guest, was the former home of Lady Gregory. All that remains of the house are some ruined walls and stables, but the grounds are magnificent, and the area is now a national park and nature preserve. "The Wild Swans at Coole" is Yeats's tribute to Coole Park:

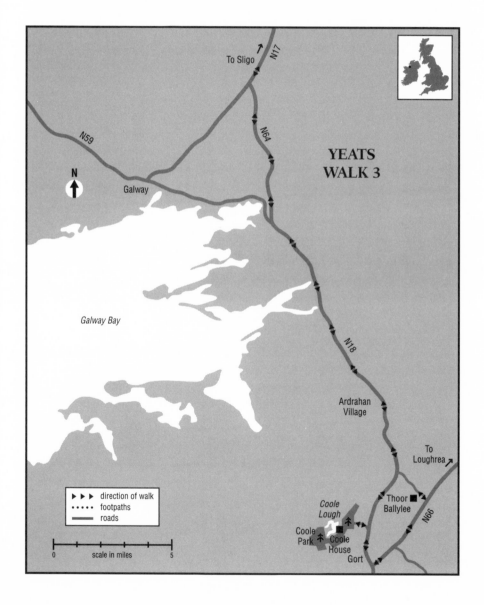

The trees are in their autumn beauty,
The woodland paths are dry,
Under the October twilight the water
Mirrors a still sky;
Upon the brimming water among the stones
Are nine-and-fifty-swans.

. . .

Unwearied still, lover by lover,
They paddle in the cold
Companionable streams or climb the air;
Their hearts have not grown old;
Passion or conquest, wander where they will,
Attend upon them still.

But now they drift on the still water,
Mysterious, beautiful;
Among what rushes will they build,
By what lake's edge or pool
Delight men's eyes when I awake some day
To find they have flown away?

A copper beech, the so-called autograph tree, stands in the park in the middle of a green expansive lawn dotted by other beech trees. Many of Lady Gregory's guests carved their initials on this beech, including Yeats and Jack Butler Yeats, George Bernard Shaw, Sean O'Casey, and John Masefield. Picnic tables are available on the grounds.

From Coole Park, return to N18 via the same road and turn right. You'll soon see a turnoff for N66; head north on this road toward Loughrea until you see a signpost for Thoor Ballylee. Thoor Ballylee, a tower that dates to the sixteenth century, is located between N18 and N66 about five miles northeast of Gort. Yeats bought this tower in 1917, the year he married Georgie Hyde-Lees, for £35 and had it restored. He spent the summers here, usually alone, for the next ten years and wrote some of his finest poems while in residence.

According to Richard Ellmann, Yeats's biographer, "The tower and many of its furnishings took on deep significance. For example, the winding stair which leads up the tower became an emblem of the spiritual ascent, with some side references to the visionary gyres, which could be conceived as the antimony of spirit and matter or heaven and earth." References to the tower are found in many of Yeats's poems, including "The Tower," "Coole and Ballylee," "A Prayer on Going into My House," "A Prayer for My Daughter," and "Meditations in Time of Civil War." In "Blood and the Moon," Yeats wrote:

I declare this tower is my symbol; I declare

Figure 18. Thoor Ballylee. Gort, County Galway, Ireland.

This winding, gyring, spiring treadmill of a stair is my ancestral
   stair;
That Goldsmith and the Dean, Berkeley and Burke have trav-
   elled there.

Yeats also wrote about the tower in letters, such as this passage from a 1926 letter to his friend Olivia Shakespeare:

> We [he and Georgie] are at our Tower and I am writing poetry
> as I always do here and as always happens, no matter how I
> begin, it becomes love poetry before I am finished with it. . . .
> As you see I have no news, for nothing happens in this blessed
> place, but a stray beggar and a heron.

You'll find one of his poems about Thoor Ballylee carved into the stone of the interior wall by the door. It is a poem Yeats hoped would survive the passage of time—"To Be Carved on a Stone at Thoor Ballylee":

> I, THE poet William Yeats,
> With old mill boards and sea-green slates,
> And smithy work from the Gort forge
> Restored this tower for my wife George;
> And may these characters remain
> When all is ruin once again.

To return to Sligo, take the road leading to Thoor Ballylee back to N66 and head south until you reach N18. Follow N18 north to where it becomes N64, near Galway. Continue north on N64 to its end, and turn off onto N17. N17 will end at N4; turn left here and continue on N4 into Sligo.

PRIMARY READINGS

Yeats, William Butler. *Mythologies.* New York: Collier Books, 1969.

———. *Selected Criticism and Prose.* New York: Macmillan/Pan Books, 1981. Includes *Reveries over Childhood and Youth.*

———. *William Butler Yeats, Selected Poems and Three Plays.* Edited by M. L. Rosenthal. New York: Macmillan, 1986.

ADDITIONAL TRAVEL INFORMATION

To call Great Britain first dial 011, then the country code, 44, then the numbers as listed below. For Ireland dial 011, then 353, then the number.

1. THE WORDWORTHS' LAKE DISTRICT

Dove Cottage and **The Wordsworth Museum:** Town End, Grasmere. Open April to September, Monday through Saturday, 9:30 to 5:30; Sunday, 11:00 to 5:30. Open March and October, Monday through Saturday, 11:00 to 4:30; Sunday, 11:00 to 5:30. Admission fee. Tel. (15394) 34455.

Rydal Mount: Rydal. Open daily, March to October, 9:30 to 5:00. Open November to February, 10:00 to 4:00; closed Tuesday; closed January 8 through February 1. Admission fee. There is a small bookstore and gift shop where entry tickets are purchased. Tel. (15394) 33002.

St. Oswald Church: Grasmere. Dorothy (d. 1855), William (d. 1850), and Mary Hutchinson Wordsworth (d. 1859) as well as other family members are buried in the churchyard.

Wordsworth House: Cockermouth. Dorothy (b. 1771) and William (b. 1770) were born in this large, stately home on the main street near the River Derwent. The home is run by the National Trust and is open to visitors. Open from April to the end of October, daily, 11:00 to 5:00; Sunday from 2:00 to 5:00. Admission fee. Tel. (1900) 824805.

2. THE BRONTËS' MOORS

Brontë Parsonage Museum: Haworth, above the Parish Church and at the end of Main Street. Open every day of the year 11:00 to 4:30; closed in January and February and 24 to 27 December. Tel. (1535) 642323, Fax (1535) 647131.

Haworth Parish Church: The Brontë family vault is inside the church.

3. D. H. LAWRENCE'S MIDLANDS

Blue Line Walk: Eastwood. See Lawrence Walk 1.

D. H. Lawrence Birthplace Museum: 8a Victoria Street, Eastwood. Open year-round, 10:00 to 4:00 November to March, and 10:30 to 4:30 April to October. Closed Christmas and New Year's Day. Regular guided tours and audio-visual presentations. Bookstore. Admission fee. Tel. (1773) 763312.

Eastwood Library: Nottingham Road. Open daily except Sundays and holidays. Excellent Lawrence display.

Newstead Abbey: Near Annesley Village. Lord Byron's home, but also a favorite walking area of D. H. Lawrence's. Beautiful grounds with peacocks, lakes, and extensive gardens. Tea shop. Open daily, April to September, 9:30 to 6:00. Gardens open year round. Guided tours of the house. Admission fee. Tel. (1623) 455900.

4. LEWIS CARROLL'S OXFORD

Alice's Shop: (for sweets), 83 St. Aldate's Street.

Ashmolean Museum: Beaumont Street. Tuesday through Saturday, 10:00 to 4:00; Sundays, 2:00 to 4:00. Free admisson.

Christ Church: Cathedral open, weekdays, 9:00 to 5:00; Sunday, 1:00 to 5:00. College open from April to September, 9:30 to 6:00; winter months, 9:30 to 4:30. Sundays, 12:45 to 5:30 (winter to 4:30). Christ Church meadow open to dusk. Admission fee for buildings.

For college openings and information obtain a copy of *A Concise Guide to Colleges of Oxford University,* a new edition of which is issued yearly (The Chapter House at Christ Church: Oxford, 1987).

5. THOMAS HARDY'S DORSET

Dorset County Museum: High West Street, Dorchester, Dorset. Open Monday through Saturday, 10:00 to 5:00, all year. Open Sunday in July and August. Features Hardy's architectural renderings for Max Gate. Tel. (1305) 262735.

Hardy's Cottage: Higher Bockhampton, Dorset. Gardens and house open from Easter until November, 11:00 to 5:00; closed Friday and Saturday. Admission fee for the house. Tel. (1305) 262366.

Max Gate: Alington Avenue, Dorchester, Dorset. Open Monday through Wednesday afternoons until 5:00. Admission fee. Tel. (1305) 262538.

6. JANE AUSTEN'S BATH

Buy a combined ticket to see the **Pump Room,** the **Roman Baths,** the **Assem-**

bly Rooms, and the **Costume Museum** at the Tourist Information Center.

The **Pump Room,** the **Roman Baths,** the **Assembly Rooms,** and the **Costume Museum:** Open daily, 9:00 to 5:00; Sunday, 11:00 to 2:00.

7. DYLAN THOMAS'S WALES

Boat House: Laugharne. Open all year, Easter to end of October, 10:00 to 5:00; November to Easter, 10:30 to 3:00. Check with Boat House, tel. (1994) 427420, or call Carmarthen District Council, tel. (1267) 234567. Admission fee.

The Dylan Thomas Centre: Somerset Place, Swansea, Wales. Inaugurated by former president Jimmy Carter. Includes a book store, exhibition hall, and events center. Open Tuesday through Sunday, 10:30 to 5:00; closed December 24 to Boxing Day (December 26). Free admission. Tel. (1792) 463980. Swansea street atlases are available at the center. The center also sponsors an annual Dylan Thomas exhibition and conference in July and August. Check with the center for details.

Dylan Thomas Writing Shed: Laugharne. Free admission.

8. JAMES JOYCE'S DUBLIN

Dublin Writers Museum: 18–19 Parnell Square North, Dublin. Exhibits of famous Irish writers, poets, and playwrights. Monday through Saturday, 10:00 to 5:00; Sunday and public holidays, 11:00 to 6:00. June, July, and August, Monday through Friday, 10:00 to 6:00. Admission fee. Tel. (1) 8722077.

Glasneven Cemetery: Finglas Road, Dublin. Joyce's parents are buried here. Open daily. Free admission.

James Joyce Cultural Centre: 35 North Great George's Street, Dublin. Joyce activities and memorabilia. Summers, Monday through Saturday, 9:30 to 5:00; Sunday 12:30 to 5:00. Winters, Tuesday through Saturday, 10:00 to 4:30; Sunday, 12:00 to 4:30; closed Monday. Admission fee. Tel. (1) 8788547.

Martello Tower, James Joyce Museum: Sandycove. Open April to October, Monday through Saturday, 10:00 to 1:00 and 2:00 to 5:00; Sunday, 2:30 to 6:00. Admission fee. Tel. (1) 809265.

National Gallery: Merrion Square West, Dublin. Open daily, Monday through Saturday, 10:00 to 5:30; Thursdays until 8:30; Sunday 2:00 to 5:00. Closed Christmas day. Free admission. Tel. (1) 6615133.

National Library: Kildare Street, Dublin. Open Monday, 10:00 to 9:00; Tuesday and Wednesday, 2:00 to 9:00; Thursday and Friday, 10:00 to 5:00; Saturday, 10:00 to 1:00, closed Sunday. Free admission. Tel. (1) 6618811.

National Museum: Kildare Street and Merrion Row, Dublin. Excellent museum. Open Tuesday through Saturday, 10:00 to 5:00; Sunday, 2:00 to 5:00; closed Monday. Free admission. Tel. (1) 6777444.

Trinity College: College Green, Dublin. Open daily. Admission fee to see the *Book of Kells*. Tel. (1) 677294.

9. YEATS'S WESTERN IRELAND

Coole Park: Open to the public daily. Free admission.

Lisadell House and **Gardens:** Open in summer only on weekday afternoons. Craft shop and refreshments served. Admission fee.

Sligo County Library and **Museum:** Library open all year. Closed Sundays and Mondays. Art Gallery open from June to September, mornings and afternoons. Free admission.

Thoor Ballylee: Gort. Open March to October, daily, 10:00 to 6:00 (until 7:00 in July and August). Tel. (91) 631436, March through October; tel. (91) 63081 the rest of the year.

GLOSSARY

alt A wooded, narrow valley or glen.

barrow A mound of earth or stones covering a prehistoric grave (see **tumulus**).

beck A small stream, usually with a stony bed.

brow A steep hill or slope; the projecting edge of a steep hill.

cairn A conical pile of stones often built as a monument or landmark.

close A field near a farmhouse; or the precinct of a cathedral; or a narrow passageway, such as an alley; or a dead end.

clough A cleft in a hill or a narrow valley.

common (or **commons**) Land used in common by a community, especially for animal grazing.

coppice A thicket of small trees and shrubs.

copse (similar to **coppice**) A thicket of small trees or shrubs; underwood or brush wood.

crag A rough, broken cliff or projecting point of rock.

cromlech A circle or oval of stones usually enclosing a dolmen or burial mound. Also a sedimentary rock found in parts of England composed of shell fragments mixed with sand.

dolmen A prehistoric monument consisting of two or more huge upright stones supporting a horizontal stone or capstone; thought to be a tomb. Found in England, Ireland, and France.

fell A rocky hillside or an elevated field without trees; frequently used in place-names.

furze A prickly evergreen shrub, often with yellow flowers.

Georgian architecture An architectural style favored during the reigns of King George I though George IV (ruled 1714–1830). It is a Neoclassical style characterized by symmetry and balance in the facades, and is influenced by the designs of the Italian architect Andrea Palladio (1508–1580).

gill A wooded ravine or glen; also a narrow stream or brook; it is also a term for ground ivy.

glade An open space in a wood or forest.

gorse Low bristly evergreen shrubs with yellow flowers found on moorland; also known as **furze**.

green An open lawn area in the center of town for community use.

grove A small wood or group of trees.

heath The various shrubgrowth on an open wasteland; or a tract of mostly treeless, open, level land covered with heather and low shrubs (see **moor**).

hollow A depressed topographical area shaped like a bowl.

kirk A church.

knob A small hill of rocks; or a rounded hill.

lough A lake.

megalith A huge stone or boulder used in preshistoric monuments (see **dolmen**).

mere A lake or pond.

moor Open, rolling wasteland, mostly treeless, covered with heather and shrubs.

parade A public walk or promenade.

pike A mountain or hill with a peaked summit.

scar A precipitous rocky place or cliff.

strand A beach; the shore.

tarn A small mountain lake.

tumulus An artificial hillock or mound to mark a grave, especially ancient ones.

weir A milldam; that is, a low dam in a river to gather waterpower to drive a mill.

wold A rolling meadow.

SELECTED BIBLIOGRAPHY

For more detailed maps of Britain, see the British Ordnance Survey Landranger Series. The maps' numbers corresponding to the areas in which the walks take place are as follows: The Wordsworths' Lake District, no. 90; The Brontës' Moors, nos. 103 and 104; D. H. Lawrence's Midlands, no. 129; Lewis Carroll's Oxford, no. 164; Thomas Hardy's Dorset, no. 194; Jane Austen's Bath, no. 172; and Dylan Thomas's Wales, no. 159.

1. The Wordsworths' Lake District

De Quincey, Thomas. *Recollections of the Lakes and Lake District Poets*. Edited by David Wright. London: Penguin Classics, 1985.

Gittings, Robert, and Jo Manton. *Dorothy Wordsworth*. Oxford: Oxford University Press, 1988.

Hutchings, R. J., ed. *The Wordsworth Poetical Guide to the Lakes*. Isle of Wight: Honeyhill Pubs, 1992.

Mahoney, John L. *William Wordsworth: A Poetic Life*. New York: Fordham University Press, 1997.

McCracken, David. *Wordsworth and the Lake District*. New York: Oxford University Press, 1985.

Nicholson, Norman. *The Lake District: An Anthology*. New York: Penguin Books, 1978.

Woof, Pamela. *Dorothy Wordsworth, Writer*. Grasmere: The Wordsworth Trust, 1988.

2. The Brontës' Moors

Alexander, Christine. *An Edition of the Early Writings of Charlotte Brontë: The Rise of Angria*. 2 vols. Oxford: Blackwell, 1987 and 1991.

Barker, Juliet. *The Brontës*. New York: St. Martin's Press, 1994.

———. *The Brontës: A Life in Letters*. New York: Overlook, 1998.

Fraser, Rebecca. *The Brontës: Charlotte Brontë and Her Family*. New York: Crown, 1988.

Gordon, Lyndall. *Charlotte Brontë: A Passionate Life*. New York: W. W. Norton, 1995.

Leeming, Gloria, ed. *Brontë Country*. London: Grange Books, 1994.

3. D. H. Lawrence's Midlands

Bennett, Michael. *A Visitors Guide to Eastwood and the Countryside of D. H. Lawrence*. Nottingham: Nottinghamshire County Council, 1975.

Chambers, Jessie. *D. H. Lawrence: A Personal Record by E. T.* New York: Knight, 1936. Reprint, Cambridge: Cambridge University Press, 1980.

Maddox, Brenda. *D. H. Lawrence: The Story of a Marriage*. New York: Simon and Schuster, 1994.

Moore, Harry T. *The Priest of Love: A Life of D. H. Lawrence*. New York: Penguin, revised, 1984.

Sagar, Keith, ed. *A D. H. Lawrence Handbook*. New York: Barnes and Noble Books, 1982.

————. *D. H. Lawrence: Life into Art*. Atlanta: The University of Georgia Press, 1985.

Tedlock, E. W., ed. *Frieda Lawrence: The Memoirs and Correspondence*. New York: Alfred Knopf, 1964.

4. Lewis Carroll's Oxford

Batey, Mavis. *Alice's Adventures in Oxford*. London: Pitkin Pictorials, 1980.

Cohen, Morton. *Lewis Carroll, A Biography*. New York: Vintage, 1996.

Morris, Jan. *Oxford*. New York: Oxford University Press, 1987.

Pudney, John. *Lewis Carroll and His World*. New York: Charles Scribner's Sons, 1980.

Wakeling, Edward, ed. *The Complete Diaries of Lewis Carroll*. Oxford: The Lewis Carroll Birthplace Trust, 1993.

5. Thomas Hardy's Dorset

Hardy, F. E. *The Life of Thomas Hardy*. London: Millgate, 1987.

Hands, Timothy. *Thomas Hardy. Writers in Their Times*. New York: St. Martin's Press, 1995.

Lea, Hermann. *The Hardy Guides*. 2 vols. London: Penguin, 1987. The original guides to the West Country approved by Thomas Hardy in 1913.

Turner, Paul D. *The Life of Thomas Hardy: A Critical Biography*. New York: Blackwell, 1998.

6. Jane Austen's Bath

Freeman, Jane. *Jane Austen in Bath*. Alton, Hampshire, England: Jane Austen Society, 1983.

Nokes, David. *Jane Austen: A Life*. New York: Farrar, Straus and Giroux, 1997.

Tomalin, Clair. *Jane Austen: A Life*. New York: Alfred Knopf, 1997.

7. Dylan Thomas's Wales

Ferris, Paul. *Caitlin: The Life of Caitlin Thomas*. Pimlico Series. London: Trafalgar Square Publishers, 1995.

Fitzgibbon, Constantine. *The Life of Dylan Thomas*. Boston: Little Brown, 1965.

Fryer, Jonathan. *Dylan: The Nine Lives of Dylan Thomas*. London: Trafalgar Square Publishers, 1995.

Korg, Jacob. *Dylan Thomas*. New York: Twayne Publishers, 1991.

Thomas, Caitlin. *Leftover Life to Kill*. London: Putnam, 1957.

8. James Joyce's Dublin

Blamires, Harry. *The Bloomsday Book: A Guide Through Joyce's "Ulysses."* New York: Methuen, 1985.

Budgen, Frank. *James Joyce and the Making of "Ulysses."* Oxford: Oxford University Press, 1972.

Delaney, Frank. *James Joyce's Odyssey: A Guide to the Dublin of "Ulysses."* New York: Holt, Rhinehart and Winston, 1989.

Ellmann, Richard. *James Joyce*. Oxford: Oxford University Press, 1983.

French, Marilyn. *The Book as World: James Joyce's "Ulysses."* New York: Shooting Star Press, 1994.

Igoe, Vivien. *James Joyce's Dublin Houses and Nora Barnacle's Galway*. New York: Irish American Book Company, 1998.

Maddox, Brenda. *Nora*. Boston: Houghton Mifflin, 1988.

Norris, David, and Carl Flint. *Introducing Joyce*. New York: Totem Books, 1995.

Thornton, Weldon. *Allusions in "Ulysses": An Annotated List*. Chapel Hill: The University of North Carolina Press, 1984.

9. Yeats's Western Ireland

Ellmann, Richard. *Yeats: The Man and the Masks*. Oxford: Oxford University Press, 1979.

Kirby, Sheelah. *The Yeats Country*. Sligo, Ireland: The Dolmen Press, 1985.

O'Driscoll, Robert, ed. *The Celtic Consciousness*. New York: George Braziller, 1982.

Yeats, William Butler, ed. *Fairy and Folk Tales of Ireland*. New York: Macmillan, 1983.

ACKNOWLEDGMENTS

The publisher and author gratefully acknowledge the following publishers for permission to reprint:

Excerpts from "Reminiscences of Childhood" included in *Quite Early One Morning*, © 1954 by New Directions Publishing Corp. Reprinted by permission of New Directions Publishing Corp.

Excerpts from James Joyce's *Finnegans Wake* used by permission of Viking Penguin, a division of Penguin Putnam Inc. Copyright 1939 by James Joyce, copyright renewed © 1967 by Giorgio Joyce and Lucia Joyce.

Excerpts W. B. Yeats's "The Black Tower," "The Man and the Echo," and "Under Ben Bulben" are reprinted with the permission of Scribner, a Division of Simon & Schuster from *The Collected Works of W. B. Yeats,* Volume 1: *The Poems,* revised and edited by Richard J. Finneran. Copyright 1940 by Georgie Yeats; copyright renewed © 1968 by Bertha Georgie Yeats, Michael Butler Yeats, and Anne Yeats.

Excerpts from "In the Memory of Eva Gore-Booth and Con Markievicz" and "Blood and the Moon" are reprinted with the permission of Scribner, a Division of Simon & Schuster from *The Collected Works of W. B. Yeats,* Volume 1: *The Poems,* revised and edited by Richard J. Finneran. Copyright 1933 by Macmillan Publishing Company, copyright renewed © 1961 by Bertha Georgie Yeats.

"To be carved on a Stone at Thoor Ballylee" reprinted with the permission of Scribner, a Division of Simon & Schuster from *The Collected Works of W. B. Yeats,* Volume 1: *The Poems,* revised and edited by Richard J. Finneran. Copyright © 1924 by Macmillan Publishing Company, renewed 1952 by Bertha Georgie Yeats.

Excerpt from "Alternative Song for the Severed Head in 'The King of the Great Clock Tower'" reprinted with the permission of Scribner, a Division of Simon & Schuster from *The Collected Works of W. B. Yeats,* Volume 1: *The Poems,* revised and edited by Richard J. Finneran. Copyright 1934 by Macmillan Publishing Company; copyright renewed 1962 by Bertha Georgie Yeats.